BLE WEED APPRECIATOR

6. BE MINDFUL OF POLLUTANTS These could include traffic fumes, storm water run-off, polluted water bodies, industrial pollutants and lead paint flaking from house walls.

7. BE MINDFUL OF HERBICIDES Ask your local management bodies whether they mark sprayed areas with signs or dyes. When in doubt, steer clear.

8. BE PERSISTENT Don't be put off by one experience with a weed that's been too tough, sour or bitter for your tastes. It may taste quite different growing in a different spot.

9. EXPERIMENT with ways to use your newfound culinary ingredients.

10. RELISH the experience!

A catalogue record for this book is available from the National Library of Australia

ISBN: 9781486320165 (pbk)
ISBN: 9781486320172 (epdf)
ISBN: 9781486320189 (epub)

Published by:

CSIRO Publishing
36 Gardiner Road, Clayton VIC 3168
Private Bag 10, Clayton South VIC 3169
Australia

Telephone: +61 3 9545 8400
Email: publishing.sales@csiro.au
Website: www.publish.csiro.au
Sign up to our email alerts: publish.csiro.au/earlyalert

Front cover: Dandelion illustration by Walther Otto Müller, 1887

Some images in this book have been modified to focus on the subject plant, remove background distractions, or show different stages of a plant (leaves, seeds, flower heads etc.) in the one image.

Cover design by MDCN Creative
Typeset by Envisage Information Technology and Adam Grubb
Printed in China by 1010 Printing International Ltd

CSIRO Publishing publishes and distributes scientific, technical and health science books, magazines and journals from Australia to a worldwide audience and conducts these activities autonomously from the research activities of the Commonwealth Scientific and Industrial Research Organisation (CSIRO).

CSIRO acknowledges the Traditional Owners of the lands that we live and work on across Australia and pays its respect to Elders past and present. CSIRO recognises that Aboriginal and Torres Strait Islander peoples have made and will continue to make extraordinary contributions to all aspects of Australian life including culture, economy and science. The use of Western science in this publication should not be interpreted as diminishing the knowledge of plants, animals and environment from Indigenous ecological knowledge systems.

The paper this book is printed on is in accordance with the standards of the Forest Stewardship Council® and other controlled material. The FSC® promotes environmentally responsible, socially beneficial and economically viable management of the world's forests.

May25_01

The Weed Forager's Handbook

A Guide to Edible and Medicinal Weeds in Australia

ADAM GRUBB &
ANNIE RASER-ROWLAND

PUBLISHING

Disclaimer

The views expressed in this publication are those of the authors and do not necessarily represent those of, and should not be attributed to CSIRO Publishing. The information contained in this publication comprises general statements based on scientific research, and is intended for educational and informational purposes only. The reader is advised and needs to be aware that such information may be incomplete or unable to be used in any specific situation. The publisher does not recommend that you rely on such information without seeking prior expert professional, scientific and technical advice.

Information in this book regarding the edibility and toxicity of plants is believed by the authors to be true and accurate at the time of writing. Readers are advised that taxonomy, nomenclature and toxicology are constantly developing and species names and knowledge about edibility and toxicity change accordingly. The book includes some common toxic look-alike species, but further toxic species are likely to exist. Foraging and consuming wild plants carries risk and readers are advised to read 'Some notes of caution' on page 5.

In particular, readers' attention is drawn to the warning that the consumption of even a small portion of some toxic plant species can cause sickness or death and that some edible species may still have toxic parts. Hence, every forager should first learn the toxic species, especially those that are potentially fatal, before foraging. If you are in any way uncertain of a plant's identity, do not eat it.

This book also discusses species that may be declared as a noxious weed, and as such, may be subject to agricultural or environmental considerations. Before growing any of the weeds in this book in your garden, check with relevant State authorities that the plant is not a declared noxious weed in the area.

The publisher and the authors accept no responsibility or liability for any harmful effects resulting from the use of the plants described herein and accept no liability for any loss, damage, or other consequences, whether direct or indirect, arising from the use or misuse of information contained in this book.

Foreword

We will fight them in the fields, we will fight them in the gardens, we will fight them in the footpaths. We will fight them why? Because someone told us to. Because someone taught us to react to a word, to a definition. Our immediate conscious action when someone mentions weeds is a reaction. And this reaction combines additional vocabulary with the word 'weed', such as 'invasive', thus building the siege mentality to the point that weeds have become a war. Weeds have become a win-at-all-costs battle that has stepped beyond the boundaries of the rules of war. There is no Geneva Convention when people enter the mindset of the world war on weeds. It's an anything goes barrage. There is no 'below the belt' when it comes to this rumble.

Weeds have been a part of my life. Growing up with a Greek heritage, gardening was a given at every residence I ever visited, be they aunts, uncles, great distant relatives, third cousins or just random Greeks for that matter. Growing was a God-given blessing and everyone grew productive and beneficial plants in whatever they could get soil into. And weeds were a day-to-day part of the plant vocabulary, the best part being that they were not seen as weeds. I always remember bus trips and picnics, and the coach or car would pull up on the side of the Hume, the Pacific Highway or by the local park and there would be all the old aunts and *yiayias* (grandmothers) walking along the side of the freeway 'emu-bob' style, pivoted at the hips and collecting every kind of so-called weed you could not imagine. When the bus stopped at the end of the trip, people lined up to pick up their bag of *horta* or weeds, call them what you like. These would then be turned into the most incredibly tasty and nutritious *hortopita* or weed pies (like spinach pie but a weed pie). Imagine the wild fresh greens, picked only an hour or two earlier being turned into that night's dinner for the family. It sings the song of reduced footprint, resilience and wild diversity in one broad brush example.

Every footpath, park or highway was not seen as some sort of grass maintenance nightmare. No no. It was seen as one big free wild salad bowl. And this is a good way of looking at this book. It is a crazy big bowl of information on plants that you would otherwise be encouraged not to consider edible, or beneficial medicinally or nutritionally. I am so pleased that more and more people are seeking out the knowledge and truths of the village and taking guided weed walks through their local area. This information and experience of the ages is getting the recognition that it duly deserves.

The book looks at the very nuts and bolts of weeds. It is a wonderful combination of scientific description, seasonally applicable take-home information, clear photographs and drawings, and equally important cultural storytelling. It reflects on weeds as colonisers. They are the mongrel street fighters that come along and re-establish life where there is only death and desolation. The capacity of weeds to set up shop and then in essence create the conditions for the next round of settlers or succession is quite remarkable. They are the true pioneers of soil building, bringing life and tolerating the torment that our technology and development inflicts. They adapt to disturbance readily, and given that we humans are such a disturbance, then it stands to reason that we go together with weeds much like a bum goes together with a pair of underpants (*kolos kai vraki* as we say in Greek).

So cast aside those weed goggles and open up your eyes and your mind to the wonderful world of weeds. As famed organic farmer Joel Salatin would put it, allow that amaranth to express its amaranth-ness. Let all weeds express their specific and unique weed-ness. Allow observation and information to open up a whole new vocabulary of wonder in the world of weeds. Don't react, rather respond to the endless possibilities that plants (formerly known as weeds) can offer you. From weekend gardener, school gardener, community and verge builders, foragers and scrumpers, urban guerrilla planters or humble rooftop and balcony farmers, this book is a must for all growers of our future food and health security. In other words, if you eat, then this book is an essential companion.

Costa Georgiadis
bLArch, compOSTA, Weed Ingester

Contents

Preface to the second edition

Fortunately for us, we still find the topic of wild edible food fascinating. In the decade or so since the first edition of this book, we've had the pleasure of meeting the profiled plants everywhere from alpine plateaus, to desert cattle stations, to urban cemeteries. No matter where we are, even in the loneliest of times, there they are! Little friends we have everywhere we go. *Edible* friends. Wild foraged weeds have been the main source of green vegetables in our diets, and we've developed ever richer appreciation and understanding of these rogue plants. We've continued learning through our own forays, culinary experimentation and research deep-dives, as well as through people we meet in person and in online spaces.

When we first released this book, we wondered if interest in re-localised urban food, including edible wild plants, might be a passing fad. As it turned out, quite the reverse has been true, with both a pandemic and concerns about global food systems in an age of climate change bringing those interests to the forefront of more people's minds than ever.

So we're delighted to be able to release a new and improved version of the book. We've added several extra weeds that we've fallen in love with, and removed a couple we thought didn't quite warrant their place at the table. There are extra cultural facts, plant-nerd facts, culinary suggestions, and better photos and illustrations to help you romp confidently into the shrubbery.

It's an honour be releasing this edition through CSIRO Publishing, whose reputation for scientific rigour meshes so well with our own goals for the book. Way back when we sat down to pen the first edition, our goal was to write something that, besides reflecting our personal experience, was also scientifically accurate – without it reading like a textbook. We were determined not to repeat misconceptions that might be circulating from some old book to a website and back to a book again. With the advantage of hindsight, we could have done better. Meanwhile, 10 years of science brings new studies and new things to report. So we've checked and updated every scientific claim in the book. A list of references can be found at www.eatthatweed.com.

In this edition we're aiming to be more precise about the imprecision of our knowledge and the state of knowledge in general. So, some of our statements (around medicinal uses in particular) are a little more nuanced and qualified – more 'suggests', 'reports' and 'possiblys'.

We've removed some less well-supported medicinal and nutritional claims, while adding some new ones, and have made some notes on our inclusion criteria for medicinal information in the introduction. On a minor note, a couple of warnings that we gave about certain plants have been removed because we no longer believe they're accurate (i.e. that older nettle leaves can irritate the kidneys – the supposed biological mechanism of this is implausible; and that chickweed contains meaningful amounts of toxic saponins – we can find no evidence of this, and some evidence to the contrary).

We're confident that our deeper experience, plus the fun we had rewriting this book, make this a more useful and stimulating read. Please enjoy, and may you find little edible friends everywhere you go!

Annie & Adam, 2024

About the authors

Annie used to make art, but noticed that the natural world was frequently outdoing her, and with greater finesse. She took up making gardens for beauty, then realised that she could feed herself at the same time. As a graduate of horticulture and permaculture courses, she has worked at several Melbourne nurseries, done urban garden design and spent time in Tanzania working on permaculture systems. A passion for questioning modern food equations led to investigating wild and other undervalued foods. She became hooked on the rich pleasures of foraging and gleaning, and hasn't stopped learning since.

Adam left a career in IT to pursue becoming backwardly mobile after a small crisis of confidence in civilisation. He started the environmental news website Energy Bulletin (now resilience.org) and began gardening, co-founding the permablitz backyard makeover movement with Dan Palmer. He's hosted the radio shows *Foodfight* on Melbourne's 3CR and *Greening the Apocalypse* on Triple R. These days he is director of the urban permaculture business Very Edible Gardens (VEG) in Melbourne. He has been roaming through the shrubbery collecting wild foods for almost two decades.

Annie and Adam have also co-authored *The Art of Frugal Hedonism* (Melliodora, 2016) and the kids' book *Let's Eat Weeds* (Scribe, 2021).

Acknowledgements

Thanks to Frances Rowland and Sarah Coles for their feedback, to Richard Camilleri for typing help, and to the dog for putting up with fewer walks.

Photo and illustration credits

We have made extensive use of botanical illustrations from archival texts. The majority have been made available thanks to the impressive efforts of Max Antheunisse, curator of www.plantillustrations.org, and Kurt Stüber at the Max Planck Institute for Plant Breeding Research (www.biolib.de).

An exception is the prickly pear illustration by Mary Emily Eaton from *The Cactaceae* (1919), made copyright-free thanks to the Carnegie Institute and www.cactuspro.com.

The angled onion illustration from *Flora Graeca* (1806) has been made available by the Sherardian Library of Plant Taxonomy, one of the Bodleian Libraries of the University of Oxford.

The wild brassica illustration from *Flora Danica* (1806) is courtesy of The Royal Library of Denmark.

The photo of Theseus and the Bull of Marathon on a terracotta pot from circa 440–430 BC, held in the Metropolitan Museum of Art, New York, was taken by Marie-Lan Nguyen, and made available under the Creative Commons Attribution 2.5 licence.

The cover illustration is from *Herbarium Blackwellianum* by Elizabeth Blackwell (1757).

Recipe photos are by Annie Raser-Rowland. All other photographs are by Adam Grubb.

Acknowledgement of Traditional Owners

This book was written on the unceded lands of the Wurundjeri and Whadjuk Noongar peoples. We acknowledge the sovereignty of all Indigenous Australians, and their deep connection to the Country on which we forage. Learning to engage with landscapes as places that provide food has given us a microscopic glimpse into how it might feel to inhabit and know a landscape as the provider of everything that you need, and for thousands upon thousands of years. We pay our respect to the peoples who are the traditional keepers of this knowledge. What has been lost is immeasurable; what remains and is being regained is invaluable.

1 Introduction: on the appreciation of weeds

There are laws in the village against weeds.
The law says a weed is wrong and shall be killed.
The weeds say life is a white and lovely thing.
Carl Sandburg (1922)

Weeds are the ultimate convenience food. They ask of you no money, no search for a parking space at the supermarket, no planting, no watering or any other maintenance whatsoever. Gathering them may call for a walk to the park before dinner. A walk that gets you a little more exercise that day, your face

A sow thistle and blackberry nightshade doing some vertical gardening.

deliciously rain-wet or your shoulders gloriously sun-warmed, and your appetite really roaring.

A remarkable number of the common weeds that sprout from Australian gardens, abandoned lots, parks and cracked footpaths are either edible, medicinal or both. Among them are some of human cultures' oldest and once most beloved food plants, as well as some of the most nutritious plants ever tested by modern science. We've documented our favourites here, in the hope that it will help you to identify, appreciate and use them safely, as free, vitamin-packed, environmentally low-impact fare.

Collecting wild foods is deeply rooted in our nature. For the vast majority of human history we have been hunter-gatherers. Even as most of our ancestors became agriculturalists, wild foods remained an important part of their diet. Reconnecting with the original function of our foraging impulses can help us satiate them before they erupt into a house full of unused kitchen gadgets, shoes or an LP jazz collection!

Foraging heightens the senses, yet is simultaneously relaxing – almost hypnotic. Urban foraging often leads you into semi-wild, overlooked places – forgotten corners and abandoned blocks where, within the metropolis, nature is reclaiming some ground.

But are weeds a rightful part of 'nature'? What is a weed anyway? Weed science textbooks offer indefinite definitions such as 'a plant that according to some human criteria, is undesirable'. In 1956 Professor William Stearn put it this way: 'Taken as a whole, weeds are not so much a botanical as a human psychological category.'

Plants once considered to be of vital cultural, culinary or medicinal importance can fall from favour and become despised 'weeds'. It's just as possible for them to traverse their way back into our sympathies. Hence, an equally valid way of doing the weeding – rather than with hoe or spray bottle – is to look past the tarnish of cultural derision,

A well-utilised manhole cover.

notice these plants' virtues, and perform a mental reclassification. For a 'valuable weed' is an oxymoron.

That's not to say we don't sometimes pull weeds from the garden – we do. But first we ask: Can I eat it? Is this plant suggesting something about the nutrient or moisture levels in this part of the garden? Is it protecting or building soil, or assisting in natural pest control? Can it make my locks look lustrous?

Given that the plants in this book all have long histories with humanity, myriad uses for them have been discovered. They tend to follow settled humans all around the world, and for a simple reason: most declared weeds are plants adapted to disturbance – including the kinds we humans are so adept at, such as clearing, ploughing and polluting. These plants have evolved to follow in our wake, and we may, by long association, have evolved the capacity to eat them. One of our staple cooking greens, sow thistle, adorns the cover of the book *The Worst Weeds of the World* (Leroy Holm, 1977). The book lists the world's 18 most objectionable weeds. A full 16 of these can be used for human consumption.

You will not get your entire diet from weeds. Most are leafy greens, high on nutrients, low on energy (so don't give up your day job just yet). However, they can be the perfect antidote for the high-energy, low-nutrition foods that characterise the modern Western diet. In extreme times, such as war, weeds have even helped avert nutritional catastrophes. Wild greens are a dense source of vitamins, and tend to have higher mineral contents and omega-3 fatty acids than cultivated greens. Cultural use of wild foods has been associated with many health benefits, not the least of which is better ageing.

In producing these free, nutrient-rich foods, no inputs are required. No fossil fuels are burnt in refrigerated trucking. No water is drained from fragile river systems. The seas are not polluted with fertiliser run-off. No birds die eating crickets that have fed on pesticide-coated leaves. It may not be possible to eat a more sustainable food.

Weeds' reputation as environmental villains might make sustainable dining seem like one bright anomaly in an otherwise gloomy scene. And while weeds can indeed be disruptive to native ecosystems and farming practices, even their bleak environmental reputation is sometimes questioned. Weeds tend to live fast, procreate a lot, and die young: characteristics of 'pioneer species' – plants adapted to colonising disturbed earth. Weeds are often those species best adapted to take hold in highly damaged ground, thereby stemming erosion, rebuilding soil structure and fertility, moderating climate and creating habitat. Where disturbances are not repeated, this process of rebuilding can eventually lead back to 'climax' ecosystems, such as old-growth forests or grasslands.

It turns out that humans, with our construction, clearing, ploughing, herbicides, water channelling, and mining, create a lot of highly damaged ground. Some ecologists now suggest that in many situations, working with rather than against weedy species, is the only sustainable way to begin repairing the (very extensive) disturbances that we have left in our wake.

Some notes of caution

Poisonous plants!

To the untrained eye, many poisonous plants are difficult to tell apart from edible and medicinal plants. Some plants are toxic even at very low doses and even some edible plants (including blackberry nightshade, which is profiled in this book) have toxic parts. Below are a few to be wary of, but naturally there are countless others. **The rule is, if you are in any way uncertain of a plant's identity, do not eat it.** Read each weed's profile closely, and see www.eatthatweed.com for our full weed photo collection, as well as guides to some common look-alikes.

Castor Oil Plant (*Ricinus communis*) With an adult lethal dose being as little as four chewed seeds, this is a plant to be super wary of. The large, lobed leaves give it a tropical look (and make it very hard to confuse with any of the weeds covered in this book). It is indeed widespread in tropical Australia, though also present throughout the rest of the country.

Hemlock (*Conium maculatum*) Once used for killing ancient philosophers – well, Socrates anyway. To the unpractised eye, hemlock's foliage could be confused with that of parsley or wild celery, and its seed heads with those of fennel. Look out for its purple-blotched stems. It is extremely toxic.

Groundsel (*Senecio vulgaris*)

All *Senecio* species should be considered poisonous, as they contain toxins that can cause liver damage. Groundsel flower buds and seed heads bear a resemblance to those of sow thistle (page 110), but the flowers have unusual triangular black dots at their bases and no petals. It is also a much smaller plant than sow thistle, and doesn't produce a white sap when broken.

Allergies and new foods

Any new food should be introduced into your diet gradually, to make sure it works well with your body, and to give your digestion time to build up the necessary enzymes. If you suffer from any existing allergies, be especially careful, particularly with plants closely related to those to which you have the allergies.

Nitrates

Several of the plants in this book appear on 'toxic plants for livestock' lists because of their ability to accumulate nitrates, especially when grown with artificial fertilisers or on un-composted manure. These include fat hen, mallow, dock, purslane and wild brassicas. Among cultivated vegetables, spinach, lettuce and broccoli are all potential nitrate accumulators too.

Nitrates cooked at high temperatures, particularly in cured meats, can form human carcinogens. Otherwise, they are considered beneficial in the diet, accounting for some of the health benefits of vegetables. However, they are toxic to younger infants, so consult a medical expert before feeding pureed greens of any kind (including your standard supermarket favourites) to children under 6 months.

Oxalic acids

Many wild edibles contain high levels of oxalic acid, notably amaranth, dock, fat hen, oxalis, blackberry nightshade, Madeira vine and purslane. Oxalic acid also occurs in many common foods, including almonds, peanuts, whole wheat, beans and chocolate, with spinach, silverbeet, sorrel and rhubarb all containing levels comparable to the aforementioned weeds.

Even if we don't eat oxalic acid, our bodies synthesise it from vitamin C and other sources. Dietary oxalic acid is an anti-nutrient though, limiting our absorption of calcium. Although rare, there are a few historical cases of fatal poisonings from excessive consumption of plants high in oxalic acid (in particular, sorrel and rhubarb leaves), as well as cases of kidney failure in people with certain pre-existing health conditions. The far more common issue is that in susceptible people, oxalic acid (and vitamin C) can contribute to kidney stones.

We use three main strategies for dealing with oxalic acid: blanch for 5 minutes and dispose of the water, or food-combine with high-calcium foods – as in our purslane recipe (page 146). The third is to be sensible. Don't let your newfound fervour for weeds lead you to eat entire buckets of fat hen in a single sitting.

Pregnancy

A special note to those who are pregnant, trying to conceive, or breastfeeding: there are warnings against consuming various herbal medicines and foods, including parsley, barberry, juniper and pennyroyal. Weeds that are not advised include oxalis, epazote and shepherd's purse. There are some doubts around nettle and blackberry nightshade too, so give them a miss if you are expecting.

Contaminants

While the plants in this book may themselves be highly nutritious, you need to be observant and use common sense when harvesting them. There are three main types of contaminants to consider: chemical (primarily herbicides and pesticides), heavy metal and biological.

Be alert for signs of herbicide wherever you are picking weeds. Some councils use a coloured dye and/or signs to indicate sprayed areas. Get to know your local area's spraying regimes if you are foraging in public spaces, and check with the council if uncertain.

Ironically, the places that get sprayed more regularly are often the places where you will find more edible weeds, as they return to fill the void that is naked ground. In areas less sprayed, the weeds are usually shaded out by longer-living species which are exploiting the soil-building effects of the weedy colonisers.

Perhaps more insidious than herbicides are industrial chemicals and heavy metals, and it is due to these that we choose not to pick weeds growing too close to urban waterways or former industrial sites. Of particular concern is lead, which has been added to our soils courtesy of lead paint, vehicle exhaust, and other household and industrial sources. For this reason, we also don't forage near busy roadways or other places where the soil might be highly contaminated with lead. Anywhere near old houses where lead paint may have flaked off or been sanded is worth thinking twice about, whether you're foraging or growing backyard veggies. Lead is especially concerning for young children as it can affect their development. The ability of many weeds to extract high levels of nutrients from the soil may correlate with higher levels of lead uptake. Despite this, plants, including weeds, are actually pretty good at *not* taking up lead. Usually, the dust on them is of more concern, so it's important to wash leaves well when harvesting in suspect areas – a dash of vinegar in the water helps remove any external heavy metals. For what it's worth, after years of almost daily weed eating, both your authors have independently had blood tests that showed negligible levels of lead.

The third type of contamination is biological. You probably got the hang of not eating faeces fairly early on in life, and while dog (and human) urine is not a major disease vector, it may not be a great salad dressing. For all the above reasons we recommend washing your weeds, particularly in the city.

General tasting notes

The first time you taste a new food, your tongue is naturally suspicious, especially of bitter flavours. Those of you who remember your first tastes of beer or coffee will know what we mean. It's often only after you eat a new food, then wake up alive and well after a night's sleep, that your tongue is willing to appreciate that food's nuances. So, if you are unsure of how you feel about the flavour at first (but are sure of your identification), do try again at a later date.

As a general note, because weeds are not bred for the human palate, choose the youngest, brightest green, and freshest looking leaves – these will be the least bitter or fibrous. Greens are also mostly tastier from plants yet to flower, and in some cases dramatically so. If you have ever grown a lettuce and tried to harvest some leaves after flowering you will well know this transformation! With regards to texture, it often helps to avoid using stems, and to chop leaves finely, against the direction of the fibres.

Medicinal notes

Many of the plants in this book have long and rich medicinal traditions. Some are gentle 'nutraceuticals', while others contain more powerful compounds – to the point of being hazardous if used without respect. Judicious use of free herbal medicines may allow you to treat some minor health problems, although we've personally had mixed results with plant remedies prescribed by alternative practitioners or found in herbalism books. In the text we make distinctions between traditional uses and those supported by scientific literature.

While studies on the medicinal uses of the plants in this book are often plentiful, many are at early stages of testing only, and so are suggestive, rather than definitive, of any relevance to human health. *In vitro* studies (those performed in test tubes) are considered a weak form of medical evidence. Because their findings may be more transferrable to external use (wound care, for example), we have referenced a couple of such uses in the book. Animal-based studies, although cruel, are considered marginally better evidence – we've noted when this is the kind of study being referenced. Randomly controlled human trials are much better evidence, and where we don't mention animal studies or the application isn't external, you can assume we are referring to these. Even these studies usually conclude with the phrase 'further research is needed'.

In summary, if you have a significant medical condition, are taking any other drugs, or have any concerns about medical effects, always seek advice from a doctor before using a plant medicinally.

Noxious weeds

A few of the plants discussed in this book are classified as noxious weeds in various parts of Australia – such as blackberry, prickly pear and Madeira vine. This means that they may be subject to restrictions, including buying, selling, displaying, propagating or transporting the plant. If you are considering planting *any* weed in your garden, check with your local council or state authority that the plant is not a declared noxious weed in your area.

2 Our top edible weeds

In compiling these notes we considered for the first time just how many species of weedy plants we personally use for food, and were amazed when the count passed 80. In this section we've listed our absolute favourites. Many are seasonal, but given that seasons overlap you can find a large number of them for much of the year. And while most are available throughout the country (and indeed much of the settled world), we admit to a small bias towards the south, because that is where we live. All the main weeds listed can be found in Adelaide, Canberra, Hobart, Melbourne and Sydney, all but one of them in Brisbane, and (subject to rainfall) all but one in Perth.

While we've included our own pictures, it's also very useful to see each plant at different stages of life and from different angles. We strongly encourage you to visit www.eatthatweed.com for additional images, and also to find details of our Edible Weeds Walks. We've included a whole heap of resources for aiding identification in the Further Resources section on page 172, including government guides, AI-based apps and social media groups – plus an invitation to send us photos via the contact form on our website if you're still not sure!

Amaranth

Amaranthus species

An amaranth in flower.

The amaranths have had a long and colourful entanglement with human cultures. They have been valued for their nourishing seeds and leaves, admired for their flowers, and religiously venerated.

Several species grow wild in Australia. One of the most common is green amaranth (*A. viridis*), but it is possible to encounter any of the varieties mentioned at the end of this section.

Green amaranth leaves can contain an astounding 38% protein by dry weight, and are store to an embarrassment of mineral nutrients. Indeed, along with dandelion, amaranth leaves are one of the five most nutritious vegetables ever tested by the US Department of Agriculture. Both leaves and seeds contain the essential amino acid lysine, which is lacking in wheat and other 'true' grains, making amaranth an excellent nutritional partner to wheat and rice.

Amaranths are largely warm-season-active plants, and in temperate climates the greens are usually best from spring to mid-summer. Pick both young tips and leaves from healthy, tender-looking plants. Due to both texture and a high oxalic acid content (see page 8), we suggest only eating amaranth cooked. Its mild and agreeable flavour makes it very versatile – try adding it to a stew, soup or curry. In Greece it is served as a simple side dish: steamed or boiled then dressed with lemon juice and olive oil, often to accompany fish.

Amaranth illustration from *Botanischer Bilder-Atlas* (1884).

While the tiny poppy-like seeds were once a venerated staple food, these days you'll mostly encounter them in supermarkets, puffed as a breakfast garnish (oh the humiliation!). Some amaranth species can bear up to half a million seeds per plant, with seed heads of a kilogram in weight. We've ground and mixed them into breads and pancakes for a delicious nutty flavour, but winnowing them is a delicate and time-consuming process.

A young amaranth, good for cooked greens.

Because of amaranth's drought tolerance, high nutritional quality and lavish seed production, this ancient plant has many times been hailed as a 'grain for the future'. News reports, however, have been equally likely to call it 'evil pigweed', for an amaranth species in the US has developed resistance to the herbicide glyphosate (as found in Roundup®), and is smothering genetically modified cotton and soya crops – much to the dismay of the Bayer-Monsanto corporation. This plant, which was once suppressed by Spanish colonists for its associations with 'pagan' rituals (see box), seems to be rising again like an ancient god to smite the crops that supplanted it!

HISTORY AND CULTURE Ancient Greeks considered love-lies-bleeding (*Amaranthus caudatus*) to be sacred and decorated tombs with it. However, the earliest archaeological record of amaranth cultivation comes from Tehuacán Puebla, Mexico, dated around 4000 BC, making it one of the oldest known food crops. The seeds were one of the staple foods of Aztecs and Incas, the latter mixing it with honey or agave syrup – and apparently, a touch of human blood – before forming it into sticky idols for communion with the gods.

A similar mix of the puffed seeds with honey, molasses or chocolate – but minus the blood – is sold in Mexico today, and called *alegría* (meaning joy or jubilation).

Look for Smooth upright stems with alternate, vaguely diamond-shaped, dull-green leaves that are rough to touch, with very apparent indented veins. The branches terminate in long cylindrical seeding spikes of various colours, depending on species – green amaranth starts out green and turns brown as the seeds ripen, while some other species have red flowers of varying shades.

Distribution Amaranths are found widely in all Australian states, though green amaranth is rare in Tasmania. All species tend to prefer full sun, and are adapted to a wide range of climates. There are native amaranth species on all continents (except Antarctica).

Relatives you might recognise The genus *Amaranthus* includes garden varieties such as the stunning love-lies-bleeding (*Amaranthus caudatus*), known for its audacious drooping red flowers and massive edible seed production, as well as Chinese spinach (*A. tricolor*) and redroot amaranth (*A. retroflexus*), both known for their edible leaves. There are several native amaranths (including *A. interruptus*) which are most common in northern Australia. They are eaten as greens and seed, and ancient remains have been found on Bunuba Country in the Kimberley, in a cave that shows signs of being continuously occupied for over 40,000 years.

A red flowering amaranth 'love-lies-bleeding' (*A. caudatus*).

Angled Onion

Allium triquetrum

Also known as Three Cornered Leek, Three Cornered Garlic, Triangle Onion, Onionweed

Originating from the Mediterranean, this pungent and delicious salad green emerges with the autumn rains. It grows lushly through winter, then produces charming white nodding bell-shaped flowers before retreating into dormant bulbs as spring heats up.

Angled onion from *Flora Graeca* (1806).

Angled onion pikelets. (See www.eatthatweed.com for recipe.)

When used raw, the whole plant – including flowers – excels as a chive or spring onion substitute. It has a sweet onion-garlic flavour as good as any cultivated *Allium*. Unlike spring onions, angled onion greens tend to squeak rather than sizzle in the frying pan, and don't caramelise readily. Nevertheless, we like to add them (chopped finely due to their fibrousness) to dishes like miso soups and omelettes. To harvest, cut whole handfuls off just above ground level. In the warmer months (provided soil contamination isn't a concern in your area), you can dig where angled onion was growing to discover the bulbs, which can be used like a less-intense garlic.

Angled onion prefers a rich, moist, well-drained soil, grows well in partial shade, and is most abundant along waterways. Since its verdant foliage and fairytale flowers make this one good-looking weed, we choose to give it a nook in the backyard to grace with its pungent presence year after year. Some people warn of this plant's rapaciousness in the garden, but we have found that as long as we vigilantly pull out the handful of self-seeded plants that pop up away from that allocated nook each autumn, it is easy to tame.

Each flower petal has a green stripe.

A pre-flowering patch. Note the ridge along the back of the leaves.

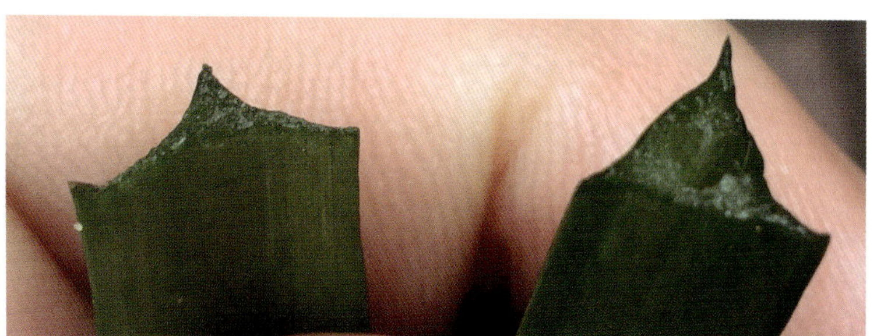

Both the leaf (left) and the flower stem (right) of angled onion are somewhat triangular in cross-section.

Look for Fleshy, bright-green leaves to 40 cm high that, from a distance, could be mistaken for grass. The leaves have a distinctive triangular cross-section. The flower stem is even more triangular and is topped with multiple drooping small white bell-shaped flowers in winter and early spring. Could be confused with the cultivated flower snowdrops (*Leucojum aestivum*), or false onion weed (*Nothoscordum borbonicum*) – but both of these have flat leaves, round flower stems, and no powerful garlic aroma.

Distribution All states except the Northern Territory, but far more common in the southern states.

Relatives you might recognise The genus *Allium* also includes leeks, garlic, onions and shallots.

Blackberry

Rubus fruticosus and relatives

This is one plant that knows how to protect its wares, and no wonder, given how utterly delicious they can be! Blackberries ripen in late summer, and should be eaten once they have turned a deep lustrous black. We prefer them sun-warmed and au naturel. However, they can be cooked in crumbles or a zillion other fruity desserts, or made into jam or cordial. If you have access to a good patch, it is easy to pick enough fruit over a season to try every blackberry recipe that tickles your fancy.

Blackberries are also somewhat of a nutritional superstar of the fruit kingdom. They are high in vitamins C and K, manganese and folic acid. But they are most notable for their antioxidants. One US study put them at the very top of a list of 1000 foods ranked by the antioxidant content found in an average serving size.

There is technique to good blackberry picking, and it's not all about wearing full motorcycle leathers. To get to those juicy berries that lie deeper within the spiny thicket, you must stomp down the highest canes in your path with your foot (wearing closed-toe

Blackberry illustration from *Kräuterbuch* (1914).

shoes of course!), using them to pin the canes beneath them to the ground. Do this with each step into the bush's centre, and you'll quickly triple your collecting area. Fruit collected very late in summer may have become home to various insects or moulds, so it is worth being a tad more observant as the season wanes.

The tannin-rich leaves and roots have been valued medicinally since at least the time of the ancient Greeks. Traditionally they are made into teas whose astringency is used to relieve sore throats and mouth ulcers, as well as diarrhoea and thrush. The leaves have powerful antibacterial properties.

Fruit are often borne at several stages of ripeness simultaneously.

NOT-SO-SWEET REVENGE English folklore once reinforced the fact that late-season blackberries can host unsavoury moulds. It was said that when expelled from Heaven, Lucifer fell square into a blackberry patch. So, each year on Old Michaelmas Day in early autumn, the devil curses blackberries, spoiling the fruit – by urinating on them!

Look for Blackberry leaves resemble those of their relative, the rose, and are a dark matte green with finely serrated edges and pale undersides. They are mostly deciduous in winter. The plant's thorny brambles grow in clumps, which enlarge as the tips of canes bend down, touch the ground and take root. In spring, small, five-petalled white flowers appear, maturing into berries that are hard and green to start with, then bright red, then the deep purple-black that tells your taste buds to get ready for a very nice time.

Distribution A European native, it is found in all Australian states except the Northern Territory. Preferring cooler climates, it is mostly restricted to areas south of Brisbane on the east coast and Perth on the west. Favoured locales include gullies, waterways, paddocks and vacant blocks.

Relatives you might recognise The genus *Rubus* also includes raspberries, loganberries (a blackberry-raspberry hybrid), cloudberries and dewberries. Blackberries are in the family Rosaceae, which also includes apples, strawberries, roses, almonds, quinces, peaches, pears, plums and apricots.

Blackberry Nightshade

Solanum nigrum

Also known as Black Nightshade

This plant is widely and incorrectly referred to as deadly nightshade in Australia – a misconception so common that we have had horrified passers-by try to 'rescue' us from eating them when harvesting in public places. The *real* – and aptly named – deadly nightshade (*Atropa belladonna) is* a somewhat similar-looking plant, but it is not naturalised in Australia.

Blackberry nightshade, a Eurasian native, was introduced into Australia as a vegetable during the gold rush. The fully ripened black berries have a rich flavour, sweet but with savoury hints of

their cousin, the tomato. They can be mixed with other fruits as a dessert, provide a sweet-tangy element in a salad, and make a fabulous addition to chutney. Early colonial cookbooks mention using them as a pie filling but, while it's easy to pluck a few handfuls as a daily treat, you'd need some patience (or some early colonists' children at a loose end) to gather enough for such an enterprise. The leaves and tender shoots are eaten widely across the globe as a cooked vegetable, and have a silky texture and a lovely rich flavour. Limiting your intake of these greens is advisable however – as with the unripe berries, there are toxicity issues to be aware of, so please read the box on page 32 and cautionary information on the following pages before use.

Blackberry nightshade has long been favoured as a medicinal plant, with mention of it dating back to the earliest herbals. Dioscorides (circa 40–90 AD), in texts that were influential for 1,500 years, recommended its leaves for treating skin diseases, earaches, indigestion and internal bleeding (definitely consult your doctor if you are suffering the latter!). *Gerard's Herbal* of 1636 reported it to be good for ulcers, ringworm, shingles and 'panic of the head'.

Chinese medicine uses juice from the leaves against the pain of kidney and bladder inflammations, and also to remedy heartburn. In Africa, the plant is widely used for several complaints, with reported successes for conjunctivitis and ulcers. Indian Ayurvedic tradition has the plant's leaves heated and applied to swollen testicles … among other uses.

A blackberry nightshade illustration from a 6th century version of *Vienna Dioscorides*.

Plants often exhibit a purple tinge.

Experiments have confirmed blackberry nightshade's anti-herpes properties, and author and herbalist Pat Collins prescribes an ointment made from the entire plant for cold sores. No human trials have been conducted, but several animal studies suggest it may have value in suppressing cancerous tumours, while also being an anti-inflammatory and having the ability to help heal gastric ulcers. Other studies suggest the plant can protect against certain poisonings of the liver – including from alcohol.

There are actually several plants, including Australian natives, in the 'Solanum nigrum complex': plants so similar they can be difficult to tell apart. The two most common are glossy nightshade (*S. americanum*) and velvet nightshade (*S. chenopodioides*), the former being native to both Australia and the Americas. Glossy nightshade has, as the name suggests, glossy berries, which are edible when fully ripe and taste particularly good. Much less is known about

CAUTION Both the leaves and berries of blackberry nightshade are eaten around the world by hundreds of millions of people from Nepal to Hawaii to Madagascar. They can, however, contain solanine and its related compounds (the green potato toxins). These toxins are only destroyed by very hot cooking (such as frying), and in parts of the world where the greens are a mainstay vegetable, processing often includes boiling them and changing the water.

When harvesting these greens, be aware that toxin levels may vary regionally, so let your tongue guide you, and reject anything that tastes more bitter than raw broccoli. Indeed, when domesticating wild potato varieties, the Aymara people in Bolivia successfully use taste to avoid those with high solanine.

When choosing fruit, stick to the fully ripened ones. These are completely black, drop easily into your hand with a gentle tug, and have no bitter flavour.

As with green potatoes, be extra cautious if you are pregnant.

velvet nightshade except that the small matte berries of this velvety narrow-leafed plant are made into jam in South Africa.

Look for A branching plant growing to an average height of 1 m, with fairly upright stems and subtly toothed teardrop-shaped leaves of a dark or even purplish-green. As it matures it develops clusters of small white starry flowers that become dangling groups of berries – initially green then ripening to a matte black.

Distribution Grows in all states, on almost any soil type, and usually in full sun.

Relatives you might recognise The genus *Solanum* also includes tomato, eggplant, potato, tamarillo and pepino.

Chickweed

Stellaria media

This is a delicate annual that grows commonly in veggie garden beds, pot plants, and wherever there is moist, rich soil. A European native, chickweed tastes, in our opinion, a little like grass, albeit pleasant grass. Some more charitable types declare it delicious, 'like young corn'. Either way, it is abundant in backyards during the cooler months, and is very good for you indeed, making it a 'superfood' and a convenience food all at once.

It is loved by chickens, who lend it their name. And they are onto a good thing: chickweed is not only high in protein, but has more than twice the iron levels of spinach, and is high in antioxidants and vitamins A and C.

We use chickweed raw in salads or sandwiches, but chopped finely because of the strong, springy fibres in the stem. Its delicate flavour comes into its own when paired with a more pungent salad green, such as nasturtium leaves. It can also be cooked (although it will substantially reduce in volume) or made into pesto.

The fibrous, springy core of a chickweed stem.

Distinctive 'mohawk' of hair on a chickweed stem.

SALAD SALON The Ainu people are the indigenous people of what is now Hokkaido, Japan. According to Ainu mythology, the first humans had bodies made of earth, spines made of willow sticks, and hair made of chickweed!

Choose lush thick stands of the plant, and harvest with scissors by snipping off the top 3–5 cm (including any flowers), as if you were trimming a beard. This method will give you more leaf and less stem, and will inspire your chickweed patch to grow a new set of lush leafy top shoots.

The classical Greeks and Romans sometimes cultivated chickweed, and it was a famine food throughout Europe until recent times. It was popular in ancient Japan, and it is still eaten in that country today as part of a symbolic seven-herb rice porridge meal. This mid-winter dish, called *nanakusa-gayu*, is eaten to promote longevity and health.

Chickweed illustration from *British Entomology* (1837).

Chickweed (left) with petty spurge (right). Don't confuse them!
(See also page 138.)

Notice the distinctly pointy tip of a chickweed leaf.

Chickweed has a long tradition of medicinal usage, most often for skin complaints, especially those that involve itching (although this does not appear to have been studied scientifically). If you'd like to give it a shot, apply as a poultice by crushing the fresh plant and securing it to the afflicted area with plastic wrap, or make an ointment by simmering a good quantity of the plant in olive oil, then straining off the oil and combining it with a little beeswax.

Look for A bright, fresh-green plant forming a low mat 5–25 cm high. It has delicate stems with a strangely elastic core, small, tender, teardrop-shaped leaves, and tiny star-shaped white flowers from late winter. The key identification tip is to look for a line of tiny hairs, like a mohawk, along the stem between nodes. Common look-alikes include petty spurge (*Euphorbia peplus*), which you certainly wouldn't want to eat (see page 138). It has a bluer tinge and produces an irritant white sap.

Chickweed flowers and bud.

Distribution Found in all states, though rare in the tropics. Prefers very fertile soil, and grows happily in full sun or partial shade.

Cleavers

Galium aparine

Also known as Sticky Weed, Goosegrass

Cleavers is a plant familiar to many people since childhood, as the whole plant is covered in fine hooks that endow it with the mischief-inviting ability to stick to clothing. Cleavers has edible seeds, stalks and leaves, and the taste is gentle and pleasant (if slightly bitter), but with the obvious drawback that the texture is not unlike Velcro. Indeed, the Middle English name for it was the overly dramatic *tongebledes,* meaning 'tongue bleeds'! As a steamed vegetable the hooked hairs soften, making it tolerable, but far better is to blend it thoroughly. Our most common usage is blending it with stock to make the foundations of a fine soup. It can also star in a green smoothie.

Native to North America and Eurasia, cleavers has a centuries-long tradition of use by herbalists, most commonly for burns and skin disorders, but also as a mild diuretic and for lymphatic complaints. Animal studies on one of its chemical constituents (asperuloside) have reported anti-obesity qualities, and cleavers' reputation on this front goes back to ancient times. Pliny the Elder reported: 'A pottage made of Cleavers, a little mutton and oatmeal is good to cause lankness and keepe from fatnesse.'

Cleavers illustration from *Flora von Deutschland Österreich und der Schweiz* (1885).

The miniscule hooks that give cleavers its clingy properties.

It has been used as an antiperspirant by the Chinese, and by milkers to strain out animal hair from milk in Sweden and elsewhere. In Turkey *Galium* species are called *yoğurt otu*, literally 'yoghurt herb', because they contain enzymes that can coagulate milk. Chickens love munching on cleavers' seeds, and the plant's other name, goosegrass, refers to the epicurean esteem in which it is held by geese. Or perhaps these fowl are chasing a buzz: cleavers is related to coffee, and its seeds do contain a small amount of caffeine. A red dye can be obtained from a decoction of the root and, when ingested, can dye bones red. We struggle to think of any useful application for that, so we'll stick to enjoying cleavers in soups.

Look for This is a bright-green, sprawling plant, with multiple long stems that climb and trail over the ground and other plants, climbing not much more than a metre. The narrow leaves are arranged in whorls of 6–9 around the stems and are covered with fine hook-tipped hairs, as are the stems. In spring to early summer, tiny green-white flowers appear, followed by pairs of seeds the size of match-heads, which are also covered in fine hooked hairs.

Distribution A common garden weed, it can be found in all states, but is rare in the tropics. It prefers moist, fertile soils and can grow in full sun or shade.

Mature cleavers, with its paired fuzzy seeds (inset).

Dandelion

Taraxacum officinale

With its toothed leaves, cheerful yellow flowers, and gossamer ball of parachuted seeds, this is arguably the most iconic of all weeds. Long valued for its reputed curative properties, dandelion has also been a much-savoured vegetable since antiquity. Several commentators suggest that it was one of the 'bitter herbs' eaten with unleavened bread in the Old Testament. Despite this bitterness, dandelion is well worth developing a fondness for – it is not only plentiful, but highly nutritious. It is particularly high in iron, calcium and vitamins A, B1, B6, E and K, making it one of the (if not *the*) most nutritious vegetable ever tested by the US Department of Agriculture!

All parts are edible. For salads, select young, fresh-looking leaves from nearer the centre of the plant. For cooking, you can be less choosy. In summer, the mildest leaves often come from those plants growing in shade. If you are sensitive to bitterness, both salt and acids (like vinegar or lemon juice) help to 'neutralise' this flavour for your taste buds. You can also chop dandelion finely and combine it with meeker ingredients. Dandelion greens complement the sweetness of root vegetables and oniony fry-ups, and pair well with rich foods like fatty meats. The flower petals of dandelions are sweetish and tender, and can be torn out and added to omelettes, patties, sandwiches or salads.

In Japan, the roots are eaten as a vegetable, but there may be technique involved as we've found them pretty tough. They do make for a tasty and popular coffee substitute though. Providing you're in an area where soil toxins are not a concern, you can harvest the roots in autumn, cut them into chunks, and roast them in a slow oven until dark brown and brittle. Grind in a spice grinder, then simmer or steep the grounds with boiling water, adding spices, milk or honey as you wish. Dandelion is a short-lived perennial, and while the best greens come from younger plants, the bigger roots come from the larger, more veteran specimens.

Dandelion illustration from Köhler's *Medizinal-Pflanzen in Naturgetreuen Abbildungen mit Kurz Erläuterndem Texte* (1887).

While the common name 'dandelion' comes from the Old French *dent-de-lion*, or lion's tooth (referring to the shape of the leaves, and perhaps also to the yellow lion's mane of its flowers), this esteemed plant's botanical name denotes other attributes. *Taraxacum* is likely derived from the Arabic word *tarakhshagog*, meaning 'bitter herb', while *officinale* is a Latin term for medicine – and dandelion does have a long tradition as a pharmaceutical. Most often it has featured in the treatment of liver diseases, kidney and spleen complaints, skin conditions and dyspepsia, and also as an appetite stimulant and digestive aid. In both Mexico and Turkey it is used as an anti-diabetes medicine.

Dandelion has been used in traditional Chinese recipes against acne, and an extract of the leaves was demonstrated to suppress the microbial activity that causes breakouts. Nobly using ourselves as

A typical dandelion, and its hollow flower stem (inset).

Dandelion leaf variations.

guinea pigs, we have tested the folk remedy of breaking the plant's flower stalk and dabbing the latex on any stray pimples, and have found them looking distinctly more sheepish by the next morning.

Humans have been spreading dandelion – both for cultivation and by accident – for so long that while it is believed to be originally from the Mediterranean, its exact origins are unclear. It is now considered native to Europe and western Asia, and is widespread on every continent (except Antarctica).

Look for Richly green, hairless leaves growing in a rosette (that is, from a central point at ground level). The shape of the leaves varies, with margins ranging from deeply toothed to only slightly serrated. These teeth tend to point back towards the base of the leaf. From the centre of the rosette emerges the hollow flowering stalk, which bears a single bright-yellow flower with densely layered petals. The flower transforms into the pale sphere of downy seeds that can be blown away by wind … or by human breath while being wished upon. The root is a taproot shaped like a slender white carrot. All parts of the plant emit a white latex when damaged.

Distribution Dandelion can be found in all states of Australia, but is less common in the tropics. It will pop up in lawns, but prefers less trodden areas where it mingles happily with lush grass at the edges of parks and pathways, or in pastures.

Relatives you might recognise Dandelion is a member of the chicory tribe of the daisy family, which includes several look-alike plants. Its most doppelganger-ish cousins are the cat's-ears (*Hypochaeris radicata* and *H. glabra*), which are hairier, have multiple flowers on each branching stalk and produce far less white sap. In any case, cat's-ears are quite edible – read more about them on page 130.

Other similar-looking plants in the tribe include chicory (page 132), wild lettuce (page 122), hawksbeards (*Crepis* species), hawkbits (*Leontodon* species), native *Picris* species, and even a couple of native dandelions (*Taraxacum* species). With the exception of this last, none of these species match all the identification features we've listed for dandelion. Fortunately, the chicory tribe is a remarkably low toxicity group of plants, and most of its weedy members present in Australia have a tradition of being eaten. Also part of this tribe is the murnong or yam daisy (*Microseris* species), whose tubers were once a staple carbohydrate for people in southern Australia. It now sadly rarely exists wild, with overgrazing by sheep and soil compaction blamed for its demise across the region. The dandelion, with its compaction-curing taproot, is now one of the plants helping to repair these degraded pastoral soils.

Fat Hen

Chenopodium album

Also known as Lambsquarters, Goosefoot, Wild Spinach

Fat hen is a summer green that grows large and lustrous in the garden. Of all the wild greens covered in this book, fat hen may be the one most interchangeable with its domesticated cousin spinach. We have received confessions from previous weed walk participants of sneaking it into dinners served to their less 'food-flexible' partners, with the only comment received being that that dish was particularly delicious that night. The flavour is mild with a slight nuttiness, the texture is silky, and it is a breeze to harvest.

While fat hen can handle dry soils and intense heat, the best picking comes from healthy-looking plants on rich or cultivated soil. We generally harvest just the young leaves and growing tips. The greens are best cooked, due to high oxalic acid content (see page 8). Steamed and served simply with olive oil, lemon juice and salt, they are superb. Fat hen is widely grown in northern India, and used in many dishes including the popular *bathua ka raita*, in which it is cooked and mashed with yoghurt and spices. Fat hen also gives spinach a run for its money in the nutritional stakes, and comes out trumps in many departments.

THE TRUTH ABOUT MELBOURNE The old English name for fat hen is 'Melde'. With that in mind, we bring you this (historically iffy) newsflash from *The Age* newspaper, 6 September 1965:

> Information on the origin of the name Melbourne has been received – rather distressing information. This fine city it appears was named after a weed whose Anglo-Saxon name was Melde *(Chenopodium album)*.
>
> The Melbourne family of Derbyshire and Cambridge, whose member Lord Melbourne gave his name to the Australian city, is itself named after the weed. Until AD 970, the name was spelt Melde-Bourne because at one time large quantities of Melde were grown in these two counties for food and fodder.

Pick fat hen leaves young.

It is particularly rich in vitamin C, riboflavin, calcium and antioxidants, and has been tested at up to 43% protein by dry weight. Body builders take note!

The seeds too, are sometimes harvested and eaten – since at least the 4th century BC in fact. Fat hen seeds were among the foods in the stomach contents of the amazingly well-preserved Tollund Man found in a Danish peatbog. Fat hen has been successfully grown from seeds found in undisturbed soil at another Danish archaeological dig; seeds believed to be 1,700 years old!

In India and Pakistan, fat hen is a traditional remedy for a range of maladies, and animal studies lend some support to its use against intestinal worms and as an anti-inflammatory.

Illustration of fat hen from *Flora Londinensis* (1775–1798).

By the time flower buds are formed, the greens are less palatable.

Look for An upright central stalk of between 30 cm and 1.5 m bears side branches with jagged-edged leaves of a dull darkish-green, often with a blue tinge. The underside of the leaves and the growth tips are coated with a waxy white powder. The green bud-clusters appear later in summer, turn red-brown as they mature, and bear tiny shiny black seeds. Fat hen could be mistaken for its edible cousin orache (*Atriplex prostrata*), which tends to grow near water and has more spear-shaped leaves. Another edible close relative is green fat hen (*C. murale*). It can be cooked in the same ways and looks quite similar to regular fat hen, but its leaves are a more vibrant green and don't have white undersides.

Distribution A European native that is well adapted to many conditions. Available across all states of Australia, usually in sunny, disturbed areas.

Relatives you might recognise The genus *Chenopodium* also includes quinoa (*Chenopodium quinoa*) and the beloved Mexican vegetable huazontle (*C. nuttalliae*). The closely related weedy herb epazote (*Dysphania ambrosioides*) is covered on page 135.

Fennel

Foeniculum vulgare

Fennel, a Mediterranean native, has been cultivated since the times of the ancients for its aromatic aniseed flavour and therapeutic qualities. Its tufts of delicate foliage often decorate sloping ground, and it seems to have a special love for the embankments of railway lines.

Try the fresh green and yellow seeds for a sweet, breath-freshening sensation that reputedly doubles as an appetite suppressant. Alternatively, let the seeds dry and grind them with a mortar and pestle for use in cooking (perfect in stews) or for making a sweet tea. Pick the very young foliage – you're looking for

A plant with lush young growth, good for picking.

Ready for the kitchen.

the stuff that is almost fluorescent green – and chop finely to use as a herb. Classic culinary tradition often finds it paired with fish, pork or beans, or used in salads, pestos and cream sauces. When used as a main vegetable ingredient, the fresh fronds – including young stems – are often boiled or slow cooked to soften their texture. *Maccu* is a traditional Sicilian broad bean and wild fennel soup. In Turkey, wild fennel fronds are cooked into a lamb stew known as *kuzu etli arap saçı*.

The wild varieties of fennel do not create a bulb like some of the cultivated ones. They do, however, make it possible for ordinary humans with ordinary bank balances to sample a rather gourmet ingredient: fennel pollen. This gold dust is gathered by swanning about shaking the flower heads of lots of fennel plants into a paper bag. You then fold it into the dough for homemade pasta, or sprinkle it over cream-tossed wild pine mushrooms in a verjuice reduction, or roll cubes of goat's cheese in it and arrange them on ridiculously large white plates ... you get the idea.

The seeds are predominant in the sugar-coated Indian seed mix *mukhwas*, eaten as a digestive after meals. Gerard reported in the early 17th century that, 'Fennell seed drunke asswageth the paine of the stomacke … and desire … to breake winde,' the latter making them quite strategic after a legume-filled curry. Fennel is an anti-spasmodic herb for the digestive system. It may be for this reason that it is part of an effective herbal mixture that helps colicky (incessantly crying) babies. An oil is extracted from the seeds, and both this and the seeds themselves are traditional treatments for chest colds. The oil also has demonstrated antifungal and antibacterial properties.

Not only do fennel's arching fronds make it very ornamental in the garden, but it also assists in natural pest control (more on this under 'Look for'). However, its clump expands readily, so give it a sunny spot in your garden by all means, but a little apart from less

Fennel flowers showing their classic 'umbelliferous' (umbrella-like) shape – a beneficial insects' utopia!

Fennel illustration from Köhler's *Medizinal-Pflanzen in Naturgetreuen Abbildungen mit Kurz Erläuterndem Texte* (1887).

vigorous plants. It lives for several years, but withers somewhat in winter, which is a good time to chop it back hard to encourage lush new spring growth.

Look for Tufts of feathery foliage that grow on stout, upright stalks. The leaves are as fine as thread, and range from vivid light green (very young) to a bold dark green (older). As with most other members of its botanical family, fennel bears its many tiny yellow flowers in an umbrella-shaped spray; a shape particularly inviting to many beneficial predatory insects including ladybirds, lacewings, and the various parasitic wasps that attack everything from aphids to codling moth. The flowers are succeeded by green seeds that mature to a pale silvery brown as summer concludes.

Be aware of the potential look-alike, toxic hemlock (see page 6). The resemblance is not great. Hemlock has none of fennel's characteristic aniseed smell, and has leaves similar to those of a carrot – quite unlike fennel's soft needles. When the plants' foliage dies back in late summer however, they are much harder to tell apart, so only harvest fennel seeds from plants with living foliage.

A sturdy fennel stem.

Distribution Found from the subtropics to cool temperate regions, in all states except the Northern Territory.

Relatives you might recognise Fennel is in the family Apiaceae, which also includes cultivated bulb fennel, dill, caraway, coriander, parsley, celery, carrot and parsnip.

Gallant Soldier

Galinsoga parviflora

Also known as Galinsoga

Dainty, approachable, tasty – yes, yes, and *yes*. But 'gallant soldier'? It seems an odd fit for this little plant. The name is actually just a mis-hearing of the genus name, *Galinsoga.* This in turn was named after 18th century Spanish royal physician, Ignacio Mariano

Younger (left) and more mature (right) gallant soldier.
Flowers and seed head (inset).

Martinez de Galinsoga, a man otherwise best known for writing a book on the health hazards of wearing corsets!

Names aside, of all the plants in this book, this one has one of the most unique flavours. Some say it tastes like artichoke. We'd say parsnip with a hint of coriander. Pick fresh-looking growth tips, including the ubiquitous flower buds. You can eat the open flowers too, but they are a bit fibrous, so are mostly best left behind. Chop your harvest finely, and eat raw in salads, or cooked in soups and stews. It's delicious when combined with cream and garlic, with fish, or in a potato salad with capers. In Colombia, it is known as *guasca,* and is the main flavouring in the popular potato soup, *ajiaco*. Colombians also dehydrate the plant to concentrate its flavour, then store it as a herb.

Gallant soldier illustration from *English Botany* (1863–1899).

With a natural range stretching all the way from California to Argentina, gallant soldier now grows in most temperate to tropical regions of the world, where it has found widespread use as both food and medicine. In Malawi, it is known as *mwamuna aligone*, which translates to 'the man is sleeping' (it doesn't have any known sedative effects as far as we can discover). It is a traditional remedy for high blood pressure in South Africa, and elsewhere has been used against diarrhoea and colds, and to promote wound healing. It has also been used to treat the bites and stings of everything from beetles to snakes to scorpions.

THE SMALLEST POSY? Gallant soldier's species name, *parviflora*, means 'little flower', and that's certainly accurate. As a daisy-family plant, its 'flowers' – each smaller than a pinky fingernail – are actually clusters of about 30 miniscule true flowers arranged in what must be one of the world's smallest bouquets! Five of the flowers on the outermost row have the distinction of producing a single white petal each.

Look for A fairly upright plant, growing to 60 cm. Its pointy, faintly fuzzy leaves are gently toothed and grow opposite each other in pairs. The plant never wastes an opportunity to branch its furry stems – indeed, at each leaf pair it splits off into more stems and flowers. Its flower heads are a mere 5–7 mm across, with a yellow centre and (usually) five, three-toed tiny white petals. The seeds are fluffy and travel by wind.

Gallant soldier has some cousins with similar-looking, if larger, flowers. A couple of these are mildly toxic when eaten raw, although we probably wouldn't recommend eating them even cooked. These plants include coat-buttons (*Tridax procumbens*), which is a low groundcover that produces long upright flower stems and grows in tropical areas of Australia. The other is St Paul's wort (*Sigesbeckia orientalis*), which has distinctive yellow petals surrounded by five sticky little green 'fingers'. Cobbler's pegs (*Bidens pilosa*), and other closely related *Bidens* species (see page 133) are also look-alikes, but happily are edible. They are distinguishable by their divided leaves and notoriously spiky seeds, and by their flowers, which tend to have either no petals or much larger ones than those of gallant soldier. Check out the look-alikes gallery at www.eatthatweed.com/weed-id/.

Distribution Gallant soldier can be found from Cairns to Tasmania. It favours warm weather, and in the subtropics it's a widespread weed of farmland and urban areas. In cooler parts of Australia, it prefers urban alleyways, cracks in concrete and anywhere else it can find warmth.

Madeira Vine

Anredera cordifolia

Otherwise known as Lamb's Tail Vine

With its lush leaves and fragrant spikes of white flowers, this vigorous South American vine was first spread by Spanish and Portuguese traders centuries ago, then continued its global travels as an ornamental specimen. It escaped into the wild, and made rather a go of it there. In certain climates (including subtropical coastal areas of NSW and Queensland), its tendrils can reportedly grow up to a metre a day, even smothering 40 m tall trees. For this reason, Madeira vine is a declared 'weed of national significance'. Biosecurity Queensland suggest that it 'has probably caused more volunteers to give up and walk away from bush regeneration projects in eastern Australia than any other weed species.' Elsewhere in the country, it tends to be a little tamer, but wherever you are, you might consider eating this invader to be something of a civic duty.

And it's well worth eating. Madeira vine has a fleshy quality to the leaves and a mild and pleasant flavour. Since discovering its charms, it has become one of our most eaten greens during the dry summer months. The large, heart-shaped leaves 'flat pack' nicely, making picking them oddly satisfying! We choose the freshest-looking leaves and bring them home stacked like a pack of cards.

In Japan these leaves are known as *okawakame*, or 'land seaweed', probably due to their viscous texture. In China they are used in stir-fries and noodle soups. In Brazil the plant's names include *espinafre-gaúcho,* or 'cowboy spinach', and it's used in salads, stews and omelettes, as well as being dried, ground and used to fortify bread. We usually eat the leaves cooked, and prefer

Note the slightly fleshy leaves.

An alleyway floral display.

them stir-fried rather than blanched, as a little crispness balances their slightly gooey nature. Chop coarsely, and toss briefly in a hot pan. They are particularly good with sesame oil, added to ramen, or simmered in a coconut-cream curry. Nutritionally, they are a good source of vitamin C and carotene. One study suggests a moderately high oxalic acid content (see page 8), although still only around half that of spinach.

Perhaps Madeira vine's least handsome anatomical feature is the lumpy aerial bulbils you find affixed to the stems. These serve as a store of energy and water in tough times, and are the plant's main means of dispersal. Beneath the soil you can find bigger tubers, and both these and the aerial bulbils are starchy and edible, like knobbly potatoes. If you happen to break one, don't be deterred by its slimy texture, as this disappears with cooking, especially roasting. They taste like potatoes too – only with even *more* lovely roasty surface area.

Madeira vine's tendrils of flowers.

Aerial tubers – ugly but delicious!

In China, one of the plant's names is *shao nian yao*, literally 'young years medicine', and the Mulao people of the Guangxi region use the leaves for 'replenishing blood'. In northern Thailand it's used postpartum to increase lactation. In its native Brazil, the leaves are traditionally applied topically for wound healing and against skin infections. In Indonesia it is known as *binahong*, and studies there have offered some support of its traditional use in treating mouth ulcers and other wounds. Here in Australia, the plant was sometimes grown en route to outdoor toilets, as it was thought to have a laxative effect. We have not independently rediscovered this quality.

A biological control agent of Madeira vine, the leaf-feeding beetle *Plectonycha correntina* had some limited releases in Queensland and NSW in the 2010s, and citizen scientists on iNaturalist.org continue to track the beetle's spread.

Look for A hairless creeper with fleshy, glossy, heart-shaped leaves that develop rippled edges in dry conditions. Its twining stems are green to burgundy when young, turning brown and woody as they mature. In summer and autumn the plant produces masses of drooping lamb's-tail-like spikes of small white to cream star-shaped flowers. The aerial bulbils appear on mature plants, and while usually around the size of unshelled peanuts, they can form messy clusters as big as cricket balls. In tropical and subtropical climates Madeira vine grows year-round, but it dies back in winter anywhere that gets a frost.

Distribution Found from Tasmania in the south to Cairns in the north, Madeira vine loves inner city fences and disturbed bushland.

Relatives you might recognise Feeling tempted to grow Madeira vine in your backyard? Don't! A non-weedy alternative would be its relative, Malabar spinach (*Basella alba)*, which looks and tastes quite similar, but lacks the aerial bulbils.

Mallow

Malva parviflora, *Malva nicaeensis* and similar *Malva* species

The ancient Romans considered mallow a delicacy, and to this day mallow species (both wild-harvested and cultivated) are widely eaten throughout the Mediterranean, Middle East, northern Africa and China. Mallow grows year-round, has a pleasant and mild flavour, and is consistently one of the most popular plants on our weed walks. Owing to the gooey 'mucilage' it contains, mallow shares a little of the ability of its relatives okra and marshmallow to thicken dishes it is cooked into.

Mallow's young growth makes for the best eating.

For salads, use the youngest leaves only. The older ones are less tender, but are better for cooking. As they age further, they often develop small yellow spots known as hollyhock rust – at which point we stop harvesting them altogether.

Cooked, mallow can stand in for spinach in any recipe, although it has more body, plus that slight viscosity which many cultures adore. In Palestine, it is known as *khobiza,* and the chopped leaves are simply sauteed in olive oil with onions, and dressed with lemon juice. We love them cooked into a curry, where their velvety texture helps to carry the flavour of spices beautifully.

The seed capsules (sometimes called mallow 'cheeses' because of their resemblance to tiny wheels of cheese) can be harvested quickly in respectable quantities when you find a large stand of plants. Choose the pale green ones that haven't yet become dry and brown, and shop around, as some species' seeds are a bit fibrous. Add them to risotto or pasta, or fry with butter, onion and mushrooms.

Illustration of small mallow (*Malva neglecta*) from *Deutschlands Flora in Abbildungen* (1796).

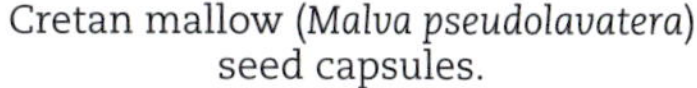

Cretan mallow (*Malva pseudolavatera*) seed capsules.

Small-flowered mallow (*Malva parviflora*) seed capsules.

Mallow is one of the earliest plants mentioned in recorded literature. In 30 BC the Roman poet Horace wrote: '*Me pascunt olivae, me cichorea, levesque malvae*' (I graze on olives, chicory and simple mallow). He believed that mallow 'develops the intellectual faculties'. Pliny claimed that 'whosoever shall take a spoonful of the mallows shall that day be free from all maladies,' and to this day there is a saying in southern Italy, *La malva, da ogni male ti salva* (mallow saves you from every disease). Dioscorides recommended mallow for the treatment of burns and skin inflammations, bowel and urinary problems, spider bites, and bee and wasp stings – uses that have persisted into modern times.

One recommendation that hasn't survived: 'Applied with urine it cures running sores on the head and dandruff.' (Check out our nettle profile for a dandruff cure that doesn't require you to put pee on your head.)

These days, herbalists utilise mallow's slimy mucilage for coughs, and to soothe inflamed throats and digestive tracts. Several animal studies have reported various mallow species to be effective treatments for gastric ulcers, and in some cases they performed better than the benchmark commercial drugs.

Mallow flower and bud.

In the garden, its deep taproot is one of nature's most talented at penetrating hard clays, leaving behind root tunnels that allow worms, air and water to begin moving through these problematic soils. Employ a few generations of mallow to start reclaiming that solid, sticky clay area in your garden.

Look for The overall shape of the lightly fuzzy leaves is somewhat like a that of a geranium, being lobed but rounded, with veins radiating out from where the leaf joins its long stalk. They are mid-green with slightly paler undersides, and softly toothed margins. Mallow flowers have five petals and range from white to pink to purple, depending on species. At 6 mm to 6 cm wide, they look a bit like little versions of the flowers on hibiscus – a botanical cousin of mallow. The flowers are followed by rounded seed capsules, which start off milky green then mature to a golden brown.

Distribution *Malva* species are natives to Eurasia and northern Africa. They can be found in all states, growing anywhere from lawns to dry embankments to moist riverbanks.

Relatives you might recognise Mallow is in the family Malvaceae, which besides the aforementioned marshmallow, okra and hibiscus, also includes hollyhock, cotton, cacao and durian. There are at least seven weeds in the *Malva* genus in Australia, as well as two native species (*Malva preissiana* and *M. weinmanniana*), both of which are known as Australian hollyhock. All are edible.

Mallow soup. (See www.eatthatweed.com for recipe.)

Nasturtium

Tropaeolum majus

Also known as Indian Cress

This South American native is beloved by many gardeners for its fiery flowers and easy cultivation. Leaves, flowers and seeds are all edible, and all share a sweet peppery flavour that is acknowledged in the name 'nasturtium', which has its roots in the Latin for 'contorted nose'. The dried ground seeds were even used as a pepper substitute in World War II.

Nasturtium illustration from *Botanical Magazine, Volume* 1 (1787).

The leaves are delicious in salads, can be used like grape leaves for making dolmades, and make an excellent watercress substitute in egg sandwiches. As kids we liked to bite off the 'tail' at the back of the flower and suck out the nectar, but grown-ups can enjoy the flowers too. They look superb on top of a salad, can be stuffed with cream-cheese mixtures if you want to make hors d'oeuvres like it's 1974, and unopened flower buds and seeds can be pickled and used like capers (see page 154). It really works!

Nasturtiums' spiciness is more pronounced when the plants are growing in heat and sun. Those spicy mustard compounds can also take credit for many of the plant's medicinal properties. It has been used in Andean herbal medicine as a disinfectant, wound healer and antibiotic, and an extract has been tested as having effective anti-inflammatory and selective antimicrobial properties.

Mexican herbalists use a topical application of nasturtium for ringworm, and also claim the plant to be good against cancer of the left lung! They might like to include the right lung too. Benzyl mustard oil, which can be extracted from nasturtiums, has been shown as effective against several types of tumorous cancers when taken orally, although only in animal studies. These mustard oils are also known fungicides, and herbalists have prescribed soaking cases of athlete's foot in a nasturtium bath. Animal studies on nasturtium tea have found it to be a powerful diuretic and treatment for high blood pressure. Random controlled human trials in Germany have reported that a blend of horseradish root and nasturtium is useful in treating urinary tract infections, bronchitis and sinusitis, and as protection against respiratory infections.

In the garden, nasturtium is considered a good companion plant, and is often planted at the base of apple and pear trees to deter codling moth.

Nasturtium flowers come in shades from pale yellow to crimson-red, or can have bicolour petals within this spectrum.

Look for A trailing, rambling or climbing plant with lush, mid-green, coaster-sized round leaves held aloft on long stalks which attach to the leaf's centre. The large gaudy flowers are orange, yellow or sometimes red, and feature a long hollow 'tail' filled with nectar. The seeds are pale-green, pea-sized grooved nuggets, often borne in threes.

Distribution Commonly a garden weed or garden escapee, nasturtium can be found in all states, often growing in urban bush, along watercourses or by roadsides. It is seldom found wild in the tropics.

Relatives you might recognise You would be forgiven for thinking that nasturtiums are related to watercress, what with watercress being a member of the genus *Nasturtium*. But they aren't even in the same family, let alone genus. Nasturtiums' common name was bestowed due to its peppery flavour being so similar to that of the cresses of the *Nasturtium* genus.

Nettle

Urtica urens

Also known as Dwarf Nettle, English Nettle, Stinging Nettle

A patch of young nettles.

Of all the weeds in this book, nettle is the easiest to identify – you can do it with your eyes closed! For anyone who has ever been stung by this plant, the spice that is revenge can only add to your enjoyment of having nettles for supper. Nettles are one of the most versatile and nutritious greens available. One modest serving of around 150 grams would satisfy your recommended daily calcium intake, and they are bountiful in protein – up to 36% by dry weight (this protein is also of a better quality than in most other leafy greens).

Illustration of nettle from *Deutschlands Flora in Abbildungen* (1796).

Nettles' feisty sting comes courtesy of tiny silica hairs filled with a mischievous cocktail, including formic acid – one of the substances responsible for the 'ouch' in ant stings. The easiest way to pick and prepare your nettles is by wearing a glove on one hand to hold the stalk, while wielding scissors or a knife in the other. As with most of the weeds in this book, we suggest skipping the oldest leaves near the bottom of the plant because they tend to be tougher.

If you do get stung, the crushed or chewed leaves of dock, which happily often grows nearby, is a traditional antidote, championed in the old English rhyme:

Nettle out, dock in –
Dock remove the nettle sting.

Blending, drying and cooking all disarm the sting. Simply blanch the leaves in boiling water for a minute, then plunge them briefly into cold water to preserve the electric green colour. Then use them without fear in your chosen dish! There are many nettle culinary classics issuing from a long Italian and Greek affection for the plant: try nettle gnocchi with sage butter (recipe on page 152), nettle and ricotta ravioli, nettle soup, nettle pesto, and nettle *spanakopita* (or more properly, *tsouknidopita*, literally 'nettle pie' in Greek). Simple nettle tea is regarded by herbalists as 'strengthening', and tastes both fresh and earthy, with slight seaweed flavours. Steep fresh or dried leaves in boiling water, or simply reserve the water strained off from cooking.

Nettle fibres have often been used to make fabric, and the whole plant to make dye – the leaves are such a vivid green that it's easy to see why. This chlorophyll-saturated hue also lends easy credence to their reputation as a blood tonic, and baskets of the plants were once hawked in the streets of London to the call of 'Nettles with tender shoots, to cleanse the blood!' Despite this enthusiasm, the poet Thomas Campbell felt nettles to be sadly underappreciated in England and wrote, 'In Scotland, I have eaten nettles, I have slept

GRASP THE NETTLE Aesop's Fables contain the advice, 'The next time you come near a nettle, grasp it firmly, and it will be soft as silk.' What's more, we have found that the dextrous can firmly (and without timidity or hesitation) pinch the leaf from beneath, fold it in half to pick, roll it hard like a little cigar, eat it raw, and exit unscathed. While performing this feat, remind yourself that you have entered not only into vegetable collecting, but into the spirit of Aesop's challenge: to embrace life fearlessly despite vulnerability.

in nettle sheets, and I have dined off a nettle tablecloth. The young and tender nettle is an excellent potherb.'

Regular ingestion of this 'excellent potherb' may reduce the pain of rheumatoid and osteoarthritis, but external application of the plant is the more notorious mode of treating sore joints and arthritis – self-flagellation with nettles is a practice that dates back at least to Roman times. The verb is to 'urticate', meaning to whip nettle leaves on afflicted areas for symptom relief. Nettle has also shown some effectiveness against enlargement of the prostate, sufferers of which will be relieved to receive the gentler prescription of nettle-root tea or capsules. Perhaps counterintuitively, nettle also contains antihistamines, and there's some evidence that consuming the leaves is a mild remedy for hay fever.

For a hair-softening and anti-dandruff tonic, steep the chopped leaves in apple cider vinegar for 2 weeks, and strain. Massage a tablespoon of the liquid through wet hair for a minute or so while in the shower, then rinse and wear those black polo necks with confidence once more.

Look for A plant of about 30 cm tall, modestly branching and upright. The leaves are a deep, bold green, have a saw-tooth edge, and grow up to 6 cm long. Green seed clusters appear at the growing tips and along the stem.

Distribution Native to Europe and northern Africa, nettle can be found in all states of Australia, preferring loose fertile soils and full sun to partial shade.

Relatives you might recognise The main weedy nettle in Australia, and the one we've been talking about, *Urtica urens,* is a cool-season annual. The less common tall nettle (*U. dioica*) is a perennial, and has pointier, coarser leaves, as does the native bush-tucker plant, scrub nettle (*U. incisa*) – be aware of the latter's even more painful hairs. The genus *Urtica* also includes the tree nettle (*U. ferox*), exclusively found in New Zealand, which has such a ferocious sting that it has killed dogs, horses and at least one person.

Oxalis

Oxalis species

Also known as Wood Sorrel, Soursob, Sourgrass

School children enjoy chewing on the long flower stems of some varieties of oxalis for the shock of sour juice – a refreshing taste that comes courtesy of the unusually high levels of oxalic acid (see page 8) contained by members of this genus, along with citric and tartaric acid. In the time of Henry VIII, the English held oxalis in great repute as an edible, but it lost favour after the introduction of the larger, leafier garden sorrel (*Rumex acetosa*), to which it is culinarily similar, but not related. We use oxalis not as a vegetable, but as a herb. This is due mostly to its intense flavour, but also to the sheer difficulty of gathering a large quantity. The leaves shrink like Alice in Wonderland

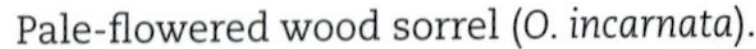

Pale-flowered wood sorrel (*O. incarnata*).

Creeping wood sorrel (*O. corniculata*) with flowers and seed pods.

when cooked, but they make a perfect tart addition to a spanakopita or an omelette or rich stew, thrown in at the last minute.

Oxalis is rich in vitamin C, and 16th century English seafarer, Sir Richard Hawkins, documented that 'diseased men such as have the scurvy, so soon as they taste the shore, eat three-leaved grass,' (in reference to oxalis). Hawkins' contemporary, Gerard the herbalist, wrote of other purported benefits: 'Greene Sauce is good for them that have sicke and feeble stomaches … and of all Sauces, Sorrel is the best, not only in virtue, but also in pleasantness of his taste.' But it is in India where the plants have been most widely used medicinally. The yellow-flowered creeping wood sorrel (*Oxalis corniculata*) has at least 80 recorded local names there! It is considered helpful in treating conditions such as influenza, urinary tract infections, diarrhoea, sprains, insect bites, open wounds, burns and hookworm.

Creeping wood sorrel was also used traditionally in India to suppress fertility in women, and an experiment on rats showed abortifacient activity. So, best avoided if you are trying to conceive.

Oxalis pes-caprae (sometimes known as 'soursob') illustration from *Hortus Halensis* (1841–1853).

One of the many purple-flowering oxalis species (*Oxalis latifolia*).

Look for Low-growing (up to 25 cm) clumping plants, with leaves divided into three heart-shaped leaflets in a vibrant mid-green. These fold up in rain, bright sunlight and at night. Different species bear five-petalled yellow, white or pink-purple flowers, which mature into small capsules. Many oxalis species could be mistaken for clover (also edible, so no concerns there), but can be distinguished by their lemony taste. Incidentally, the Irish aren't bothered which one you call the Shamrock, as long as it has the three wee leaves.

Distribution *Oxalis* species are available throughout the continent in a wide range of climates and conditions, though those lush enough to pick usually appear in moist or semi-shaded spots.

Relatives you might recognise The genus *Oxalis* also includes oca (*Oxalis tuberosa*). Also known as New Zealand yam, it produces a small edible tuber which is readily available in greengrocers and supermarkets in that country.

Plantain

Plantago species

Also known as Ribwort

There are several common species of these most useful plants, the most abundant being the strappy-leaved common plantain (*Plantago lanceolata*). In damper spots you may encounter the larger oval leaves of the greater plantain (*P. major*), and in mowed parks, lawns and drier areas you may find the small, ornately formed leaves of the buckshorn plantain (*P. coronopus*). The latter is cultivated in Italy for its mild nutty flavour, but the leaves

Common plantain (*P. lanceolata*) (below and opposite).

of wild specimens are generally too small to be rewarding. The greater plantain variety does provide more foliage, but both it and common plantain have a slight flavour of bitter mushrooms. This can actually become a complementary note to other tastes, but is overbearing on its own, so choose the tenderest young leaves, and use them in a mixed salad, soup, stew, stir-fry or smoothie.

Psyllium powder is made from the seed husks of some cultivated varieties of plantain. These husks are abundant in soluble fibre and are used in commercial preparations (such as Metamucil) to soothe the digestive tract, improve bowel regularity, and reduce the absorption of cholesterol. You can try eating the seed heads of the wild and weedy varieties chopped onto your breakfast cereal for similar effect.

The leaves are prized medicinally. Anglo Saxons called plantain the 'Mother of Herbs', and included the leaves as part of their Nine Herbs Charm, used for treating poisons, cuts and infections (both nettle and fennel also feature in the concoction). In Norway, common plantain is known as *groblad*, and on the Isle of Man it is *slan lus*, both essentially translating as 'healing herb'. The leaves and their juice are widely used on wounds of all types. They have

Common plantain illustration from *Flora Batava*, Volume 1 (1800).

demonstrated antibacterial and anti-inflammatory properties, and contain bio-regulating proteins that may indeed give the plant wound healing abilities. All you have to do is chew up a leaf and *voilà*, you've made a ye olde 'spit poultice'. Some human trials have given support to its use on skin ulcers and in ulcerative colitis.

A LITTLE ETHNOBOTANY So closely has the proliferation of common plantain followed the spread of agriculture that archaeologists look for its fossilised pollen to estimate the expansion of early Neolithic farming throughout Europe. Almost 10,000 years later, when Europeans reached the Americas, greater plantain followed their movements in such a predictable fashion that indigenous peoples branded it 'white man's footprints'.

Buckshorn plantain (*P. coronupus*).

Greater plantain (*P. major*).

Look for Members of this genus are easiest to recognise when in flower, as their leaves vary a great deal. Most have oval leaves (either wide and fat or long and narrow, depending on the species) growing from a central point on the ground. These are dull green and softly hairy, with a coarse texture and parallel veins. A cylindrical flowering spike that looks a little like that of a miniature grasstree appears on a stalk poking up from the plant's centre, browning off as the seeds mature.

Distribution The three plantain species mentioned can be found in all states except the Northern Territory, and not in the tropics of any state. Usually found in full sun, often in compacted ground, they will tolerate heavily trodden areas, including pastures and parks.

Prickly Pear

Opuntia ficus-indica

Also known as Indian Fig, Nopal

With its heady mix of succulent fruit, gorgeous flowers and wicked spines, prickly pear is an important plant in its native Mexico, where it is used heavily as fruit, drink and vegetable. Known locally as *tuna*, the fruit are sold on the streets pre-peeled and stuck three to a wooden skewer, as well as being made into jellies, candies and jams, or transformed into several brands of liquor. They have a

Ripe fruit. Beware of the insidiously tiny needles known as 'glochids'.

flavour somewhere between persimmon and kiwifruit, and seem somehow even more sweet and refreshing for the unlikeliness of having come from a spiny cactus.

The pads are known as *nopales*, and are eaten in tortillas and tacos, cooked with scrambled eggs, or served as a side with beans, rice and other dishes. They are delicately tart, and taste very much like themselves in a way that you get a yen for once you have experienced it a few times.

If you don't have a talented Mexican cook to gather and prepare your cactus for you, don't be disheartened! Let's start with the fruit. These duck-egg-shaped baubles appear on the rims of the cactus pads, starting off green then maturing to orange or deep purplish-red over the course of summer. Ripe fruit are tender to squeeze. They lack the large spines found on the pads, but they *do* have tiny hair-like spines called 'glochids', which can be very irritating if stuck in you, so you need sturdy gloves to pick and prepare your fruit. Native Americans rolled them in coarse sand to get rid of the glochids, so you could give that a go, but we generally just use a knife to slice them open, and then spoon out the brightly coloured insides. Perform this task while wearing gloves, and in a spot where fallen spines can be disposed of easily (over a very large plate or outdoors).

The pads (or 'paddles') have both big naughty-looking spines and, in some varieties, also a modest serving of the tiny, insidious glochids – in these cases they should also be prepared with gloves. Use a knife to trim off the rims of the paddle, and shave the spikes off its surface, then wash your utensils, chopping board and the paddle clean of spines. You can now handle it like any other vegetable. Cut it into strips or dice it, and fry until tender. If you want a softer texture, pre-boil the pieces in salted water for 5–8 minutes – this also allows you to lessen the 'slimy' factor that

A STUDY IN CRIMSON In the 16th century, prickly pears provided Mexico with its biggest export after silver, and it had nothing to do with food, but with glamour. The *Opuntia* cacti are the chosen home for the scale insect *Dactylopius coccus*, which produce a red acid in their bodies that can be made into the crimson dye cochineal. The world beyond the Aztecs had not encountered such a hue before, and it became a hugely important commodity until the arrival of the synthetic dye industry. Nowadays cochineal – also known as carmine – is mostly used in cosmetics and food colourings, where its status as a 'natural' product is maintaining its popularity.

Prickly pear (*Opuntia ficus-indica*) illustration from *The Cactaceae* (1919).

comes from prickly pears' sap. Many people love this okra-like texture, but if you are not one of them, you can even change the boiling water part way through, or add a pinch of bicarbonate soda for the last 2 minutes of boiling. *Over*cooking increases the sliminess and destroys the crispness that is part of the cactus' charm.

Dress your cooked paddle pieces with lime juice, olive oil and crumbled feta, sauté them with other vegetables, or use them as a topping with chilli and kidney beans for a brave new pizza Mexicana (see our recipe on page 160). Alternatively, skip the chopping and boiling, and score them halfway through in a criss-cross pattern, brush with oil and seasoning, then grill gently until they start to soften and char just a little. The young pads picked in spring are traditionally regarded as the best, having the mildest flavour. Older pads can become quite fibrous.

Young pads, perfect for eating.

There's some evidence that eating prickly pear fruits before drinking alcohol (... tequila anyone?) can reduce the severity of a hangover! The cooked paddles have been found to reduce blood sugar in several small human trials, suggesting that their traditional Mexican use against diabetes may be on point. As in mallow, plantain and purslane, the 'slimy' element in prickly pears' texture arises from mucilage, the soluble fibre that helps soothe upset digestive tracts and irritated throats.

Look for Hard to miss this one: dull-green oval cactus pads the size of badminton racquets covered in 1 cm spines. The pads generally cover the stem thickly, and the plant can be up to 3 m tall, often forming tangled clumps that arise when old paddles drop to the ground, take root and form new plants. The large, yellow, cupped flowers are borne in rows along the paddles' rims from late spring, before becoming fruit as summer progresses.

Distribution *Opuntia ficus-indica* occurs across all states, usually in full sun and in settled areas. Other *Opuntia* species are available across the continent, particularly in dry areas. In urban areas they are most often found by the back fences of gardens they have escaped from, frequently along train tracks and creek embankments.

Relatives you might recognise You may come across many related *Opuntia* species, including *O. stricta,* which was once a widespread threat to NSW and Queensland farmers. Efforts to control it included the slaughter of many tens of thousands of emus, magpies and crows – which ate the fruit and spread its seed – until, famously, the introduction of the cactoblastis moth as a biological control. All *Opuntia* species can be eaten, but with varying degrees of effort depending on their flesh-to-thorns ratios.

Purslane

Portulaca oleracea

Also known as Wild Portulaca, Pigweed, Munyeroo

Purslane's glisteningly fresh little leaves leap out from bare and disturbed soil in spring. Relish it while it is available over the warmer months, for its crisp, tart succulence makes it a culinary delight. Purslane is used extensively in Middle Eastern and Mexican cuisine as both a raw and cooked vegetable. Its tangy flavour complements tomatoes, feta, roasted pumpkin, beans, fish, hard-boiled eggs … the list could go on. We harvest it by plucking the growth tips (with or without flowers and seed heads) and the larger, younger leaves. Avoid picking too much stem if using it raw, however cooking softens them nicely.

Purslane has been referred to as a 'superfood', for it is the richest source of omega-3 fatty acids of any leafy greens ever tested, and is high in protein, potassium, vitamins A, C and E, and antioxidants. It was eaten by European explorers of Australia's interior to stave off scurvy, with botanist Ferdinand von Mueller declaring, 'I have reason to attribute the continuance of our health partly to the constant use of this valuable plant.'

It has been ranked as the eighth most common plant in the world, and its range is truly global. It is considered native to everywhere from North Africa to Indonesia, and while not often described as native to North America, seed deposits show it beating Columbus to the 'New World' by at least a millennium.

As you may have gleaned from von Mueller's experience, it is also native to Australia, where it has been an important food source for Indigenous Australians throughout much of the continent, from Victoria to the Kimberley. The roots were cooked and the greens and stems eaten fresh, but perhaps of most value were the tiny seeds, which were a staple, particularly in arid areas. Victorian colonist Robert Smyth wrote in 1878 of them being baked into cakes 'infinitely superior to cakes made of nardoo flour'. Nineteenth century botanist Joseph Maiden concluded that 'the

Purslane (including seed capsule detail) illustration from *American Weeds and Useful Plants* (1865).

ZESTY CHEMISTRY Purslane is one of the only plants in the world to have two different ways of photosynthesising. Normally it uses the fairly common 'C4'-style photosynthesis. But in dry conditions, it can switchstyle photosynthesis. But in dry conditions, it can switch on the cacti-style of doing things, known by the mouthful 'crassulacean acid metabolism', or just 'CAM'. CAM-based plants only open their stomata (the little breathing holes in their leaves) at night, which helps them retain water during the day. Problem is, this forces them to collect and store all the carbon dioxide that they'll need for the next day, during the night. Their trick is to transform it into malic acid, a zesty tasting liquid. By morning they are full of it, and they gradually use it up throughout the daylight hours. The take-home? If it's dry where you live, your purslane will be tarter in the mornings than in the afternoons, and you can choose when to harvest it based on your flavour cravings!

Purslane with and without flowers.

food prepared from this seed must be highly nutritious', noting that the Maijabi people of Cape York call it thukouro, and 'get in splendid condition on it'. Purslane is another plant high in oxalic acid, so check our note of caution on page 8.

Medicinally, it has long been used for its proven abilities as an anti-inflammatory, an analgesic and a wound healer, so it is great for bumps, sprains and scrapes of all kinds as a topical application. Herbalist Pat Collins calls it her 'summer chickweed' (purslane is available in the warmer months, chickweed in the cooler) for she uses it freshly crushed as a poultice on hot and itchy skin conditions.

Look for Fingernail-sized, semi-succulent, mid-green oval leaves on plump stems, which are greenish-bronze to start with and then become quite red. The young plant has large leaves on stems that reach upwards (to 20 cm), but as growth continues the leaves produced are smaller and the plant tends to lie on the ground like a lacy mat. Tiny yellow flowers appear at the growing tips and in the fork between leaf and stem, and produce thousands of seeds like black grains of sand.

Distribution Purslane has an amazingly even distribution across the continent, from Tasmania to the dry centre to the Torres Strait Islands, with a tendency towards full sun and disturbed and bare earth. It seems to like growing in the cracks between loose paving, though seldom to a size worth picking from.

Relatives you might recognise Purslane is in the family Portulacaceae, which also includes the larger, domesticated purslane subspecies golden purslane (*P. oleracea* subsp. *sativa*), the dwarf jade plant (*Portulacaria afra*), as well as several ornamental portulacas found in nurseries.

Salsify

Tragopogon porrifolius

Also known as Purple Salsify, Oyster Plant, Goatsbeard

A recently emerged salsify, a potential root harvest specimen.

Salsify is also known as the oyster plant, as within the fleshy taproot of some specimens there can be discerned a seafood-like flavour. We've tried it baked, fried and boiled, and it certainly is delicious, although we are yet to stumble across any oysterish notes. Sixteenth century herbalist Gerard declared it 'a most pleasant and wholsome meate, in delicate taste farre surpassing either Parsenep or Carrot'. In the name of vegetable kingdom egalitarianism however, we will choose to describe it as 'equal to any of the popular pointy roots, and a little like the love-child of parsnip and artichoke hearts, yet milder'.

The roots are harvested in winter or spring before flowering, after which they become too fibrous. They snap quite easily upon tugging, so gently does it – or use a trowel. They look like slightly disoriented, small white carrots. The harder the soil, the more likely they are to fork into confusion; it's in softer soils that you'll find more rewarding examples. Give them a scrub with a stiff brush, peel off all knobbly or hairy bits and trim the ends, and they are quickly brought to order, ready to cook. Both leaves and roots exude a milky white sap when cut, but this has none of the bitter flavour you may expect, though it does cause root pieces to discolour

A wild salsify root.

very quickly, so drop them into a bowl of water spiked with lemon juice until you're ready to cook them. Keep it simple by steaming the pieces then sautéing in a little butter and soy sauce, or parboiling then roasting with olive oil, bay leaves, coarse salt and some smashed cloves of garlic. Or follow tradition and make them into a gratin, croquettes, fritters or a cream of salsify and mushroom soup. They can become simultaneously mushy and fibrous if overcooked, so aim for tender but not collapsing.

A flowering salsify plant, looking less grass-like and more branched due to maturity.

Harvesting the growth tips in spring.

As with dandelion and chicory, you can also roast the root to make a coffee substitute. Also, the root latex can be used as chewing gum. File that under things to keep you busy after the collapse of civilisation. Only harvest root crops where there is no reason to suspect soil contamination.

The young shoots can also be collected as a treat in spring. We remove some of the grass-like part of these shoots, and fry what remains quickly, as you might asparagus – which they are not unlike, though arguably superior!

In 18th century Britain, salsify went through a period of popularity as a root vegetable, and it is still cultivated on a small scale in Europe and Russia. Varieties with larger roots are available, such as the eccentrically named 'Mammoth Sandwich Island'. Gardeners sometimes also plant it for its hardiness and striking flowers.

The seed head with its wind-riding mini-parachutes.

Look for Salsify appears in spring as a 'basal rosette' – its dull-green, grass-like leaves grow from a central point on the ground. It's at this stage of life when it is best harvested as a root crop, but is hardest to recognise. Later, the upright stems and flowers appear, reaching up to 1 m in height. These muted purple, 3–5 cm wide, daisy-type flowers are made distinctive by having bracts (the spikes of the green cup that hold the flower) that are longer than the flower's petals. The seed head is not unlike that of dandelion, only larger. One commentator, seeing salsify for the very first time (next to a train line in Poland), entertained the theory that they might be dandelions 'genetically modified in some way by electromagnetic forces from the pantograph cables'. The plant exudes white latex if damaged.

Distribution A native of southern Europe and northern Africa, salsify can be found south of the tropics in all states of Australia except the Northern Territory. It prefers full sun and can handle dry conditions. Perhaps a less common weed than others we've mentioned, but a special treat. Look out for them in grasslands, roadsides and vacant lots.

Relatives you might recognise Yellow salsify (*Tragopogon dubius)* is a very similar plant, only with yellow flowers, which can be used in the same ways. Spanish salsify (*Pseudopodospermum hispanicum*), available in seed catalogues, is a relative with a black-skinned taproot which is considered excellent eating.

Salsify illustration from *Bilder ur Nordens Flora* (1901–1905).

Sow Thistle

Sonchus oleraceus

ALSO KNOWN AS MILK THISTLE, SMOOTH SOW THISTLE, PŪHĀ, BUCKABUN, DALURP

A young plant, good for salads.

Sow thistle's species name *oleraceus* announces its edibility! Or would if you spoke Latin – it's derived from the word for 'vegetable'. And this is one widely eaten vegetable. From Malta to China to Māori societies, there are local names and recipes for this plant across time and geography.

The leaves, which are rich in vitamins, iron and calcium, have an agreeable, albeit slightly bitter flavour. We'd say they taste like lettuce, only *more so*. The bitterness intensifies in older plants, but diminishes when cooked. The growth tips – including not only the leaves, but the delightfully crisp hollow stems and the unopened flower buds – are excellent stir-fried, steamed or added to soups. From mature plants pick the top 15 cm or so of growth – if it snaps off cleanly, it will be delicious chopped, sauteed and dressed with olive oil and lemon. For salads, use tender leaves from young plants (include a scattering of the yellow petals too, if you like). With its ubiquitousness, ease of harvesting and enjoyable flavour, sow thistle takes the coveted number one spot on our personal list of most eaten weeds!

Harvesting growth tips of older sow thistle for cooking. Note the white sap and hollow stem.

Before harvesting, check for aphids, some species of which adore plants of this genus. But don't fret: these types of aphids generally only attack sow thistle, whilst simultaneously luring beneficial insects like ladybirds into your garden.

If you've never seen a sow thistle before, you may think us a little overly devoted to eating wild foods in this case, but *Sonchus* species are not true thistles and have no painful spikes (the 'sow' part of their name relates to the fondness pigs have for them). We grew up calling this plant 'milk thistle' – a tribute to the white latex it exudes when broken. The plant more properly called milk thistle however, *is* a true thistle: the medicinal plant *Silybum marianum*, which is covered on page 137.

Sow thistle has a long and wide history of medicinal use. A 13th century English herbalist recommended a diet of sow thistles 'to prolong the virility of gentlemen', no doubt boosting the plant's popularity in the late Middle Ages. Pliny recommended it for bad breath, and famous 17th century herbalist

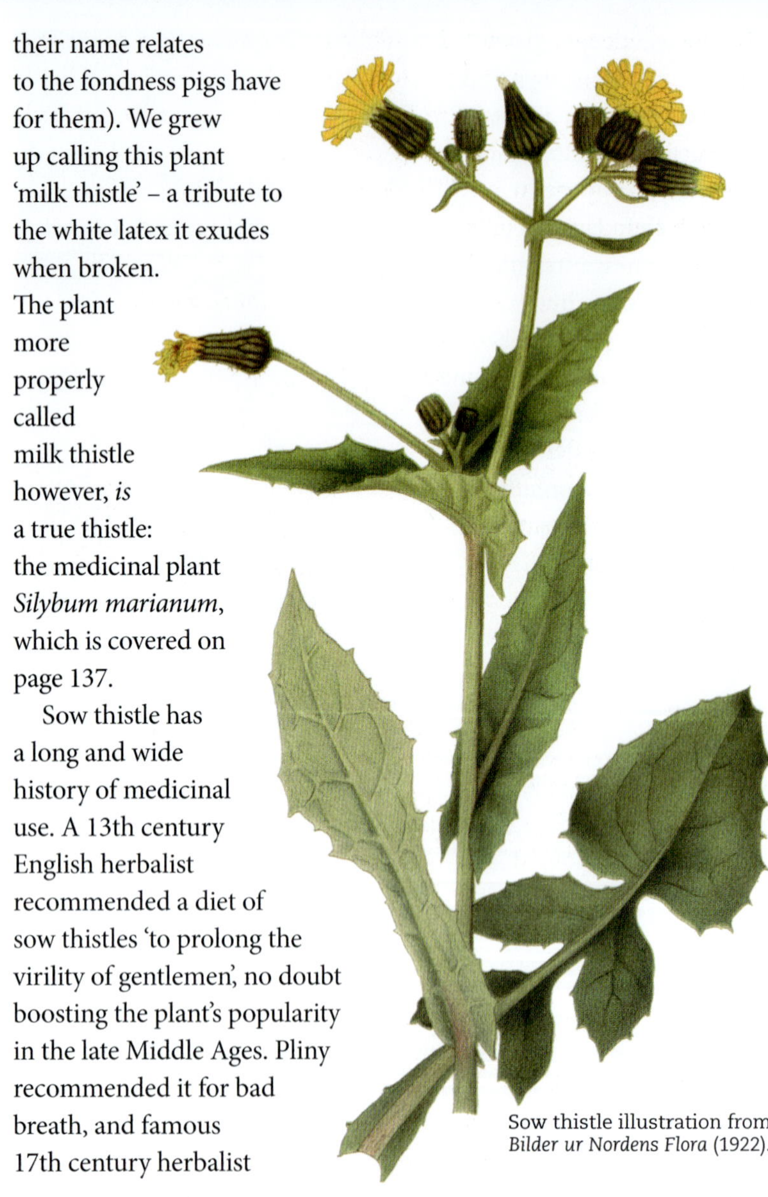

Sow thistle illustration from *Bilder ur Nordens Flora* (1922).

Nicholas Culpeper promoted its milky sap for cosmetic uses, noting that it 'is wonderful good for `women to wash their faces with, to clear the skin and give it lustre'. Based on the 'doctrine of signatures' (the belief that plants can be used to cure ailments of body parts they resemble), Culpeper wrote, 'The decoction of the leaves and stalks causeth abundance of milk in nurses, and their children to be well-coloured.' Animal studies have suggested it may be useful in treating diabetes and ulcerative colitis, and as an anti-inflammatory.

Many European explorers of Australia mention seeing and eating sow thistle, and representatives of the Yorta Yorta people and leading ethnobotanist Beth Gott consider it to be native – although that view remains contentious. At the very least, and perhaps due the presence of edible native relatives, Indigenous Australians were quick to adopt sow thistle as food. In the Yorta Yorta language it is known as buckabun, and in Woiwurrung it is dalurp. In 1878 Smyth reported the Gunaikurnai spiritual belief 'that the soul, as soon as it leaves the body, goes off to the east, where there is a land abounding in sow-thistles ... [in] which the departed eat and live.'

DIY SUPERPOWERS In an ancient Greek precursor to Popeye's spinach popping, Theseus, the mythological founder of Athens, strengthened himself with a bowl of sow thistle before his encounter with the Bull of Marathon. E.C. Segar, the creator of Popeye, chose to promote spinach not because of its iron content as is popularly believed, but because of its high vitamin A content. Either way sow thistle is higher in both carotene (the vitamin A precursor) and iron than spinach, so Theseus chose the better vegetable.

Note to kids: Eat your greens before fighting bulls (and remember your pants).

Look for This plant is a shape shifter: it changes dramatically as it matures. And yet we have found that our Edible Weeds Walk participants rapidly pick up on the progression after seeing a few plants at different growth stages, and rarely have trouble identifying it successfully. Perhaps this is testimony to our many millennia of plant observation in the name of survival. When young, the tender leaves are a misty matte green and have a spade-shaped tip, followed by one or more smaller arrow shapes. As the hollow stem elongates and begins to branch, the leaves become more jagged, coarser, and slightly shiny, often with a blue undertone, and the plant looks more like an upwardly mobile dandelion. The yellow flowers, too, are dandelion-like, and also turn into pale, fluffy

seed heads, although they never form a complete sphere as with dandelions, and multiple flowers are born on the stalks instead of just one. By the time seeds develop, the plant can be up to 1 m tall, and often has a purple tinge. One potential look-alike you'll want to avoid is groundsel – see page 7.

Distribution A native to Eurasia, sow thistle is one of the most widespread weeds of the world. It occurs across a wide range of conditions and throughout most of Australia.

Relatives you might recognise A close relative, prickly sow thistle (*Sonchus asper*) is also widespread, and is traditionally used interchangeably with common sow thistle for medicinal purposes. Prickly sow thistle is also edible, but has more thistle-like leaves. There are two native species that are also close relatives (*S. hydrophilus* and *Actites megalocarpa*), both used by Aboriginal peoples as food.

Wild Brassicas

Brassica species

Also known as Wild Cabbage, Wild Mustard

A patch of Mediterranean cabbage (*Brassica fruticulosa*).

Weeds are the perfect candidates for domestication. Their short generations and bountiful seed production make developing desirable characteristics relatively easy. Some notable examples of this come from the cabbage or *Brassica* genus, several species of which were taken from the wild and cultivated by ancient farmers. Over the centuries, these European and Asian agriculturists bred these plants into root, seed, flower and leaf crops in a fantastical array of peculiar forms – from Romanesco broccoli to kohlrabi. The ancient Greeks grew three *Brassica* varieties, and Greek mythology reports that the cabbage first sprouted from where Zeus' sweat hit the ground. This may account for the slightly sulphuric aroma of cut cabbage, but it tastes surprisingly nice considering …

Wild *Brassica* species abound, with eight in Australia alone. Broccoli, cauliflower, kale, Brussels sprouts and cabbage are all cultivated forms of *Brassica oleracea*. The wild cousin that your authors eat most frequently is Mediterranean cabbage (*Brassica fruticulosa*). The young plants look almost indistinguishable from broccoli seedlings, and the taste is pleasant and immediately familiar, although sometimes with notes of mustardy warmth or bitterness, so it can be worth taste-testing before harvesting (or serving as a side dish so that diners who don't love these flavours can choose how much to have).

In slightly wetter areas you may find the larger-leafed wild turnip (*Brassica rapa*). This is the same species as wombok, bok choi and turnip, but one that has escaped cultivation several times and re-wilded itself. You might also encounter liberated siblings of Indian mustard (*B.* × *juncea*) and black mustard (*B. nigra*), whose fiery flavour infuses not only their seeds, but their leaves too. In Nepal and the Punjab region of India and Pakistan, these greens – rather than spinach – are the traditional ingredient in saag-style curries.

Wild cabbage (*Brassica oleracea*) illustration from *Flora Danica* (1806).

Distinctive seed pod and flowers of the *Brassica* genus.

Other species, like the dryland specialist Saharan mustard (*B. tournefortii*) may not be as tasty – it's a little tougher and hairier – but all *Brassica* species, and all parts of the plants are considered edible. Wild brassicas come in all textures, shapes and colours (well, green to purplish-green …) but since none are toxic, once you know the basic identifying features, you can go forth, taste and experiment!

We have a soft spot for the buds and yellow flowers, which are like teeny broccoli heads you can nibble on while foraging, or add to a salad. Unless very soft and young, the leaves are generally best cooked – many develop a lovely velvety texture. Cook into Asian noodle soups, pan-fry with potato, onions and haloumi, wilt with poached eggs and tomato relish – how you use this leaf will vary according to variety, but if you think of a 'cabbage to mustard greens' flavour spectrum, the classic culinary accompaniments will do you nicely.

A young wild turnip (*Brassica rapa*).

Harvested growth tips of Mediterranean cabbage, ready to chop and cook.

There's little nutritional data available specifically for *wild* brassica varieties, but brassicas in general are a good source of many health-promoting substances including folic acid, carotenoids, selenium, organosulphur compounds and vitamin C.

Medicinally, the *Brassica* tribe is perhaps most studied for its anti-cancer properties. Regular consumption is associated with reduced lung, colon, prostate and other cancers. Eating brassicas may also assist in preventing diabetes and lowering blood cholesterol.

In the garden, mustardy brassicas are an excellent natural pest-control agent. Chop the plants roughly with a shovel and dig into the soil in spring as a 'bio-fumigant' for up to 40% more produce from your *Solanaceae* crops (e.g. potatoes, tomatoes and eggplants), particularly if you have grown these in the same spot the year before. The technique is even used on commercial farms, offering an alternative to banned synthetic pesticides such as methyl bromide.

Look for Wild brassicas are a motley crew, but are united by their four-petalled yellow flowers growing at the tips of the flowering stalk. Before they open, the flower buds cluster like a tiny head of broccoli. After they flower, they leave behind a spray of elongated seed pods (up to 7 cm long in some species), which are similar to miniature pea pods. A papery strip is left behind after the seeds and pod fall away. Most *Brassica* species have deeply lobed and ripple-edged leaves.

Distribution Collectively, the wild brassicas have a wide distribution across all states and climates, but are less common in the tropics. They are adapted to disturbed soil of all types, and grow in full sun.

Relatives you might recognise There are many look-alike relatives in the greater Brassicaceae family which could be confused with true brassicas. Happily, we can find nothing to suggest any are toxic in ordinary quantities, and many are widely eaten and quite delicious.

These relatives include the widespread wild radish (*Raphanus raphanistrum*), which has lightly bristled leaves, and flowers which vary from pale yellow to white. Its fresh greens cook up surprisingly well. Wild rocket (*Diplotaxis tenuifolia*) is a spicy salad treat for those of us in the southern states, often found in dryer spots. Sea rockets (*Cakile* species) are a salty, wasabi-flavoured relative found from the subtropics down to cool-temperate coastlines. Charlock (*Sinapis arvensis*) could easily be confused for a true brassica, but it too is edible and very pleasant. The hedge mustards (*Sisymbrium* species) are peppery relatives that could also be mistaken for true brassicas. They have long been used for food and medicine, but they do contain low levels of a heart stimulant so probably shouldn't be eaten in excess.

Wild Lettuce

Lactuca serriola

Also known as Prickly Lettuce, Opium Lettuce

Wild lettuce is a lovely delicate green, and the wild ancestor of cultivated lettuce. Its taste is indistinguishable from that of its descendants and it can be used in just the same ways. Being sturdier than many lettuces, it is also suitable for cooking. For

A young wild lettuce, good for eating.

An older plant, past its prime for eating.

raw use, pick from the low-growing young plants (mostly found between autumn and early spring), as this is when the leaves are most tender, crunchy and mild. Past this appetising stage, the plant undergoes quite a Jekyll-and-Hyde transformation. It grows an upright prickly central stalk, and the leaves become increasingly leathery, bitter and spiny! That said, the growth tips are soft enough that they can be harvested and cooked, using tricks to minimise bitterness as per dandelion.

Wild lettuce illustration from *Flora Regni Borussici* (1844).

When cut, the plant weeps a white latex known as lactucarium. This has analgesic and sedative qualities, for which it gained the name 'lettuce opium' (despite containing no true opiates). Hippocrates described these mild narcotic effects in 430 BC. Pliny, in the 2nd century, wrote of the lettuce's ability to suppress sexual desire. Yet, paradoxically, the ancient Egyptians used wild lettuce for just the reverse – as an aphrodisiac. Italian ethnobotanist Giorgio Samorini believes he has found the answer: 'Tests showed that 1 gram of lactucarius induces calming and painkilling effects because of the presence of lactucin and lactucopicrin … At the highest doses [2 to 3 grams], the stimulating effects of tropane alkaloids prevail. This finally solves an ethno-botanical riddle.' Way to go science!

Wild lettuce seeds and flower.

The distinctive row of hairs along the back of the spine of a young leaf (above). These become even more pronounced on the bitter leaves of older plants (below).

Look for When young, the mildly serrated leaves grow in a 'rosette' – radiating from a central point at soil level – and the plant looks a little like a brighter dandelion. Each leaf has a single row of stiff hairs running along the midrib on the leaf's underside. As it ages, the plant forms a strong upright stem, the leaves stiffen and take on a darker, bluish tinge, the leaf hairs become hard and prickly, and small yellow flowers are produced. The whole plant exudes white latex when broken at any age.

Distribution Native to Europe and Asia, it is found throughout Australia, from Hobart to the tropics. It grows widely, in conditions ranging from desert to garden to shady riverbank. The tastiest plants grow in moist, fertile soils and often in partial shade.

3 | Other weeds of note

Plants included in this section have definite merits but are generally less common, harder to harvest or process, or offer some other impediment to free and easy enjoyment by comparison with those that made our main list. Some are medicinal-only or have poisonous parts, so don't go eating just any bits that take your fancy. This short selection far from covers this wide country's other weedy edibles and medicinals. It is merely a taster. As with the main weeds, you can find more photos of these plants at www.eatthatweed.com.

Briar Rose

Rosa rubiginosa

Both the petals and the hips of this wild rose can be used in cooking. Jellies, jams and syrups are favourites. Briar rose hips are tastier than the fruit of most cultivated roses, and homemade rosehip tea is as simple as simmering 7–10 hips in water for 5 minutes. The hips should be collected in summer and autumn

when they are deep red and soft. Use the whole hip if you are simply extracting its 'vital essences', as for syrup, jelly or tea. But if you are making jam or using the actual flesh in other ways, you will have to split the hips and scrape out the seeds and hairy fibres that surround them, as these are an intestinal irritant. The flowers of this prickly shrub are modest by cultivated-rose standards, featuring a single row of pink petals. They are found in the southern states extending into southern Queensland, and grow as a weed of roadsides, grazing land and disturbed bushland.

Calendula or Pot Marigold and Field Marigold

Calendula officinalis and *C. arvensis*

Commonly planted as vegetable garden companions, both the leaves and flowers of these unfussy plants are edible. We prefer the very young leaves, cooked. The petals have a slightly peppery sweetness and, apart from being great raw as a salad ingredient, they can be used in fritters, broths or creamy dishes to add flavour and impart a gorgeous golden colour. Feed them to your chooks for egg yolks so yellow you'll need sunglasses when dunking your toast soldiers in them. Traditionally used (with some scientific support) for anti-inflammatory and wound healing properties, they are often made into salves and ointments for use on burns, cuts and chapped skin. Calendula is mostly a garden escapee, while field marigold is a more widespread weed of fields and wastelands.

Cat's-ear and Smooth Cat's-ear

Hypochaeris radicata and *H. glabra*

Cat's-ears are often mistaken for their cousin dandelion, but they have two main distinguishing features: roundly lobed leaves and multi-flowered, branching flower stems. Their leaves are also coarser and hairier, especially those of *H. radicata*. Cat's-ears aren't eaten as often as dandelions, perhaps because of this hair, but they are actually less bitter and make quite a decent cooked green.

In turn, cat's-ears are often confused with hairy hawkbit (*Leontodon saxatilis*), whose single-stem flowers droop coyly in the bud stage before standing upright to open. Fortunately, hairy hawkbit is also edible! A white-flowering cat's-ear (*H. albiflora*) grows in parts of New South Wales and Queensland. We haven't been able to find any records of its edibility, but it is unlikely to be toxic.

Chicory

Cichorium intybus

This bitter green shape-shifter can be used cooked and in salads in much the same way as its cousin, the dandelion. The roasted roots have been made into a coffee-style drink for centuries. In Australia, chicory is both a garden plant and a widespread weed, especially of fields and roadsides south of the tropics. It can look somewhat like a dandelion with more upright leaves, although just as commonly the leaves are smooth-edged, lacking the dandelion-like toothing. Most weedy chicories we encounter have a characteristic fuzz on the back of the midrib, however some varieties lack this too. The give-away is its distinctive sky-blue flowers on branching stems – but even here you may occasionally find them in white!

Cobbler's Pegs

Bidens pilosa

Cobbler's pegs, also known by a range of curse words, is notorious for its long black seeds, which stick to trousers and shoelaces. Yet this scrambling South American native is one of the most important wild greens in eastern Africa. You can add the tips and young greens to soups, though the resinous taste is not to everyone's liking (only one of us enjoys it). These greens are high in antioxidants and have many uses in folk medicine, including using juice for gastric ulcers and as a wound dressing. Cobbler's pegs is widespread in Australia, but less so in the south. Look for the distinctive 'sea urchin' seed clusters, and small white-and-yellow daisy flowers – though the petals on these are sometimes absent.

Docks and Sorrels

Rumex species

Sheep sorrel.

Dock.

Plants from the large *Rumex* genus are referred to as either docks or sorrels. They are all edible, but with flavours ranging from scrumptious to unbelievably bitter. When good, these plants are a delicious, strongly lemony cooking green. Pinch off a corner to test-taste before you bother picking. Sheep sorrel (*Rumex acetosella*), with its small fish-shaped leaves, is the most consistently good. It often grows on acid soils and in pastures. Its larger cousins, the various docks, are particularly prevalent near waterways and on heavier soils, and vaguely resemble a thinner-stalked silverbeet. All are high in oxalic acid (see page 8).

Epazote

Dysphania ambrosioides

Despite smelling somewhat like turpentine, this Central American native is a mainstay herb in Mexican cooking. An upright plant growing to a little over a metre, it bears some resemblance to its relative fat hen (page 48) but with narrower, greener and sometimes sticky leaves, and – once you learn it – that unmistakeable aroma. We've come to love it. Epazote leaves are used to flavour soups, rice dishes, enchiladas and sauces, but most commonly, bean dishes, where they are thought to reduce the flatulence beans can provoke. They are an irreplaceable ingredient in authentic refried black beans. Epazote is very pungent – use it as a herb, not a vegetable. Strong infusions and essential oils of the plant can actually be poisonous, especially for young children or during pregnancy and breastfeeding. Epazote can be found from Victoria to the tropics, usually along the banks of creeks and rivers.

Groundcherries

Physalis species

There are currently eight species of *Physalis* (known collectively as groundcherries) that grow wild in Australia. The most well-known of these is the cape gooseberry (*Physalis peruviana*), followed closely by tomatillos (*P. ixocarpa* and *P. philadelphica*). Groundcherry species can be found throughout all non-arid areas of the country, and all have edible fruit. They often taste like tangy tomatoes and are excellent in salads and salsas. This is true, too, of the piquant cape gooseberry, but unlike the other groundcherries, it is most often eaten in desserts. The fruits are enclosed in a distinctive 'lantern', which turns papery once the fruit inside is ripe. Parts of the plants other than the ripe fruit can be mildly toxic, including the bitter, underripe green fruit, and the enclosing lantern. Most other groundcherries' leaves aren't as furry as the cape gooseberry shown in the photo, but all species have fused-petal flowers similar to the one shown and lanterns enclosing the fruit.

Milk Thistle

Silybum marianum

This is an intimidatingly spiky thistle with dramatic white markings – almost as if milk has been splashed on it. It is considered a liver tonic, and is commercially available as such in capsule form. An extract of the plant is used for treating suspected liver poisoning from the death-cap mushroom (*Amanita phalloides*). There are indications it may be a good complementary medicine for treating other liver conditions and type 2 diabetes. Milk thistle is widespread, but is more common in the countryside than the city. The name milk thistle is also sometimes applied to sow thistle (*Sonchus* species, see page 110).

Petty Spurge

Euphorbia peplus

Not to be eaten, this diminutive and fragile-looking weed produces a fiercely skin-burning white latex when cut. An extract of petty spurge has been developed commercially for treating actinic keratosis (the flaky pre-cancerous 'sun spots'), however there are more effective medications. It can be used to treat warts though. The home user should dab a drop of the sap onto the affected spot once or twice a day, washing off any that ends up where it shouldn't. Be *very* careful not to get any near your eyes. Petty spurge is very common and found in most gardens, anywhere from southern Queensland to Tasmania.

Shepherd's Purse

Capsella bursa-pastoris

The little heart-shaped seed pods of shepherd's purse have a peppery-mustardy taste, while the edible leaves and flowers are milder. All are good in salads. It is widespread, and often grows in parks and ovals, where mowing means this small plant is kept even smaller, making the seed heads the best fare. It is traditionally used for stopping both internal and external bleeding – on one of our walks, an elderly German woman remembered collecting it for soldiers during WWII. A small study supports its use in reducing menstrual blood flow.

Stork's Bill

Erodium cicutarium

The young leaves of this geranium relative taste a little like carrot tops. They are best chopped finely and cooked. Musky stork's bill (*E. moschatum*) is an equally common, close relative with – as the name suggests – a faint musky aroma. It is difficult to distinguish between the two species, but both are edible. These plants can be prolific in pastures and expanses of mowed grass, and grow widely in regions south of the tropics.

Sweet Violet

Viola odorata

The flowers of all violets are considered edible. They can be made into syrups, added to salads, frozen into ice cubes for summer drinks, or used crystallised in cake decorations. In cities, the most common variety is sweet violet, which likes damp, fertile, shady places, and can be found in all the capitals except Darwin. It has mild leaves which can be eaten raw when very young; otherwise they can be used cooked, and have a slightly thickening effect in soups, similar to mallow. Some sources mention the seeds and rhizomes of violets causing gastric discomfort and other symptoms, so avoid these parts.

Wild Celery

Apium graveolens

Wild celery is the same species as cultivated celery. Sometimes, weedy versions are recent garden escapees, while others have spent longer re-wilding, and have thinner stalks and a fabulously potent flavour. Chop stems and leaves finely for a memorable salad experience or for use in soup stocks. Wild celery is usually found near creeks and streams, so avoid it if water contamination is an issue. It is a minor weed of urban areas, and is not found in the tropics.

4 Weedy recipes

These recipes aim to hit the mark on several levels: they are delicious, easy, healthy and economical, much like the weeds they feature. We have also tried to work with ingredients that many people will already have in their pantries – a practical homage to the foraging concept of using and enjoying what is right in front of you rather than buying specialty products to fit a whim.

Recipes are a great starting point when discovering a new food. Use them to get a feel for the weeds' individual charms, then disregard them and cook as your palate dictates! There are suggestions for use (both traditional and our own) dotted through the profile of each weed for further inspiration. You can also find more weedy recipes at www.eatthatweed.com.

Green Smoothie

Want to eat some free health food? Without the need to masticate? This may be the recipe for you. Call it Monster Powers Juice and it is a brilliant way to get kids to eat a big serve of greens. For the slightly more mature amongst us it also seems to do quite a nice job on a mild hangover. Mix it up by adding grated ginger or chopped mint.

Ingredients for 2 serves

1 medium banana (frozen is especially nice)
1 medium orange or half a mango – or use a whole mango and skip the banana
1 cup of water
about 1 cup, depending on taste, of mixed weeds: chickweed, cleavers, dandelion (keep this one to a minimum if you're sensitive to bitter flavours), mallow, nettle, plantain and sow thistle all work well.

Avoid fennel, nasturtium and more than a skerrick of purslane in this recipe, as their strong flavours will take over.

Method

Wash and de-stem all the weeds, and chop across the grain. Peel and slice the orange, removing any pips, and break the banana into chunks. Place all ingredients in a blender and whizz until smooth.

Purslane Yoghurt Dip

This is essentially a variation on tzatziki, and in all earnestness we declare it a superior one. If you plan on kissing someone who hasn't shared this with you, you may want to add half a cup of finely chopped flat-leaf parsley to offset the effects of the garlic (also add a little extra yoghurt and olive oil in this case). Otherwise, experiment with adding a tablespoon of very finely chopped wild fennel, dill or mint.

Ingredients for 4 serves

- 1 tightly packed cup of washed purslane, stems mostly removed
- ½ cup good-quality plain yoghurt
- 2 cloves of garlic, minced
- ¼ teaspoon salt
- 1 tablespoon extra-virgin olive oil

Method

In a bowl, mix together the yoghurt, oil, garlic and salt, then fold through the chopped purslane. Put in the refrigerator to chill. Serve with hunks of fresh bread.

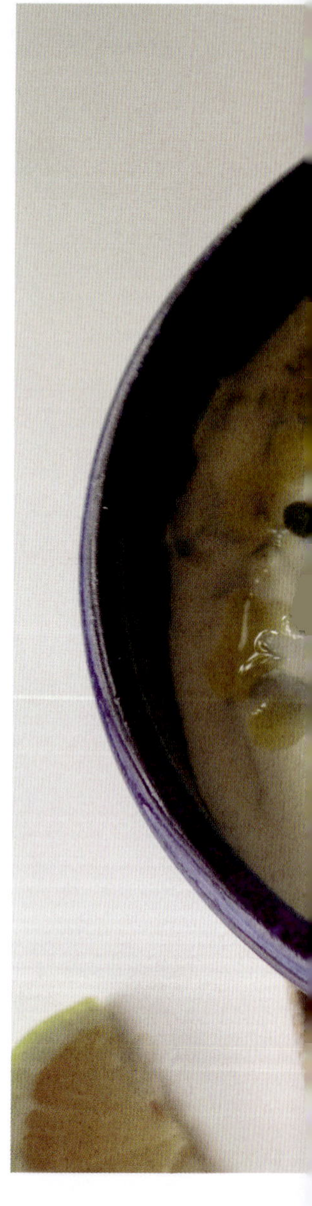

Mixed Weeds Salad

This is pure, nearly unadulterated weedy goodness. The nutty crunch of seeds plus the sweetness of the sultanas really help to set off the flavours of the wild greens, and even the cynical polish this off with lip-smacking fervour during our edible weeds cooking courses. It looks very nice too.

Chickweed, dandelion, wild lettuce and nasturtiums are wonderful inclusions when in season. For mallow, plantain, sow thistle and wild brassica, pick the youngest, most tender leaves for salad eating. You can also add purslane and a little angled onion or fennel, both chopped very finely so as not to dominate.

Ingredients for 4 serves (as a side dish)

3 tablespoons mixed sunflower and pumpkin seeds (pepitas)
2 tablespoons sultanas
6 teaspoons tamari
4 tablespoons extra-virgin olive oil
2 tablespoons balsamic vinegar
2 tablespoons lemon juice
salt and pepper to taste
mixed weeds – enough to fill a large salad bowl
petals of 3 calendula flowers (or other edible flowers – wild brassica or nasturtium flowers are delicious)

Method

Toast the sunflower and pumpkin seeds with the sultanas in a dry pan over a low heat. As they begin to colour, sprinkle with 2 teaspoons of tamari, and keep stirring gently until they are coated and the liquid has evaporated. Allow to cool completely.

Mix the olive oil, remaining tamari and lemon juice in a small jar and shake well. Add salt and pepper if desired.

Wash and de-stem all weeds, pat dry thoroughly, and chop across the grain. Toss in the bowl with the dressing.

Sprinkle the toasted seeds, sultanas and calendula petals over the top immediately before serving.

Weedy Frittata

Frittatas were surely invented as a glorious way to use up a glut of eggs by wrapping them around a glut from the garden – or around some tasty leftovers. Add sliced steamed potatoes or diced roasted vegetables to make this even more of a meal. For glamour, decorate the surface with thin circles of tomato or strips of roasted capsicum just before popping it under the griller.

Fat hen and nettle (see page 81 for tips on handling) both go exceedingly well with eggs. The bitter note of dandelion is lovely here, and amaranth, mallow, plantain, sow thistle and wild brassica are all good inclusions too.

Ingredients for 4 serves

1 tablespoon olive oil
6 eggs
¼ cup milk
¼ cup grated parmesan
1 teaspoon rosemary, very finely chopped
1 teaspoon sweet paprika
salt and pepper to taste
1 cup angled onion (Don't use the top two-thirds of the leaves, as these become fibrous with cooking. If not in season, substitute with 1 clove of garlic plus onion or leek.)
4 cups mixed weeds
½ cup grated cheddar

Method

Keeping angled onion separate, de-stem and wash all weeds, and chop across the grain. Steam all but angled onion until just tender, then squeeze out excess liquid.

Whisk the eggs, milk, parmesan, rosemary, salt and pepper together in a bowl.

Heat the oil in a heavy-bottomed frying pan, and fry the angled onion with a pinch of salt until softened. Stir the weeds evenly through the egg mixture, then pour it over the angled onion in the frying pan. Swirl paprika through the mixture with a fork. Reduce to a low heat and cook for 5 minutes, or until mostly set.

Sprinkle cheddar over the top, and put the pan under a griller on low heat. Cook until the cheese has melted and turned golden – takes about 3 minutes. (Tip: if your frying pan has a wooden or plastic handle, wrap a little foil around it where it will be exposed to the griller.)

Nettle Gnocchi

These little dumplings are a nettle classic. Walnuts pieces are sometimes added to the sauce in this sage butter version, while a mixed-herb cream sauce with a splash of brandy is also excellent.

Ingredients for 4 serves

The gnocchi

- ½ kg or 3–4 medium floury potatoes
- 150 g nettle leaves (about 3 cups, fairly firmly packed)
- ⅔ cup grated parmesan
- 2 free-range egg yolks
- 1–1½ cups of plain flour, plus extra for rolling
- salt and pepper to taste

The sauce

- 2 tablespoons olive oil
- 2 tablespoons butter
- 3 tablespoons chopped fresh sage leaves, or 2 of mixed thyme and rosemary
- 3 cloves of garlic, finely chopped

Method

The gnocchi Peel and chop the potatoes, steam until tender, then mash until smooth.

Drop the nettles into a pot of boiling water for 2 minutes, then transfer them to a bowl of iced water for another 2 minutes. Drain and squeeze out the excess water with your hand. Chop very finely then stir into the potato mash.

Add half the cheese and both the egg yolks, and season well with salt and freshly ground black pepper. Add 1 cup of flour and quickly work it into the potato mixture. When the dough feels not too sticky to roll out, cut off a small piece, roll it into a ball and drop it into boiling water to test. If it floats to the surface after a minute or so and holds its shape well, your dough is ready. Otherwise incorporate a little more flour and test again.

Generously flour your work surface and roll the dough into long sausages about the thickness of your finger, and cut off pieces 2 cm long. As you go, keep the gnocchi on a tray with a little flour sprinkled over them.

To cook, drop batches into a large saucepan of boiling water. Be careful not to overcrowd the pot, or the gnocchi will stick to each other. They are done when they float to the surface (generally within a minute). Remove with a slotted spoon and tumble them in a little olive oil to prevent sticking.

The sauce In a pan, melt the butter with olive oil, and fry the sage and garlic until just crispy, then stir in the gnocchi to warm them through.

Sprinkle with the remaining cheese to serve.

Egg and Nasturtium Sandwiches

This is a punchier twist on that proud member of the Sandwich Hall of Fame, the egg and cress sandwich. You could use true capers, but using nasturtium 'capers' is more fun because it turns the sandwich into a nasturtium theme party!

Nasturtium capers are simply the plant's pickled flower buds and seeds. Choose totally unopened buds, and seeds that are still fresh and green. Measure your seeds and buds in a cup, and bring the same volume of white wine vinegar to the boil with a good pinch of salt and a few smashed peppercorns. Then pour this hot mix into a jar over the 'capers'. You can add a bay leaf, dill or tarragon if you like. Seal and leave for at least a month.

Ingredients for 2 serves

2 hard-boiled eggs
2 tablespoons mayonnaise
½ cup nasturtium flowers and young leaves (in equal parts)
1 tablespoon chopped angled onion
1 tablespoon chopped nasturtium 'capers' (for recipe, see above)
salt and pepper to taste
4 slices of very good bread

Method

Chop the eggs and nasturtium leaves and flowers finely. Combine them in a bowl with all the other ingredients (except the bread!) and mash with a fork until well mixed. Apply to bread.

Moroccan Mallow Stew

Mallow is a much-loved wild green in the Middle East and northern Africa, and is frequently paired with coriander, garlic and lemon. *Bakoula* (mallow puréed with red olives and preserved lemon and then used to dunk bread in) is a classic Moroccan dish.

The following recipe is a mallow-y variation on another classic, *harira.*

Ingredients for 4 serves

5 cups tightly packed young mallow leaves, de-stemmed and washed
⅔ tin or 1 cup cooked chickpeas, drained and rinsed
1 tin or 1½ cups cooked chopped tomatoes
zest of 1 lemon, plus the juice
3 cloves of garlic, minced
1 teaspoon salt
3 tablespoons chopped dates or sultanas
2 teaspoons each of ground coriander and cumin
large pinch of chilli flakes
2 tablespoons extra-virgin olive oil
1½ cups couscous
½ cup good-quality plain yoghurt
4 tablespoons flaked almonds

Method

Roughly chop the mallow leaves, and place all ingredients except the oil, almonds and couscous in a deep pan with a heavy base. Simmer covered for 10 minutes, then uncover, stir and simmer for a further 2–3 minutes. Stir the oil through immediately before serving.

While the stew is cooking, toast the almonds in a dry pan until pale brown.

Boil 2 cups of water with a big pinch of salt. Take off the boil, pour in the couscous, stir, and cover with a lid for a few minutes. Remove the lid and fluff with a fork.

Place mallow mix on a bed of couscous. Add a dollop of yoghurt and sprinkle with toasted almonds to serve.

Wild Cabbage and Eggplant Stir-fry

This is an unabashedly pan-Asian, unabashedly scrumptious vehicle for the tangy, mustardy medley that is oxalis and wild brassica. That said, you could use any of the cooking greens mentioned in this book instead, but we think this combo has the most kick for offsetting the creamy mildness of the eggplant and tofu.

Ingredients for 2 serves

1 tablespoon sesame seeds
1 small eggplant
4 cups firmly packed wild brassica greens, washed, and chopped roughly across the grain
1 cup firmly packed oxalis leaves, washed
a small knob of ginger
2 cloves of garlic
1 small red chilli
1 tablespoon oil – coconut or peanut is ideal
2 teaspoons sugar dissolved in 3 tablespoons tamari
1 teaspoon sesame oil
200 g firm tofu, cut into 5-mm thick slices, or 2 small fillets of mild white fish
¾ cup jasmine rice (about 2½ cups when cooked)

Method

Toast the sesame seeds in a dry pan on a low heat, and set aside. Start cooking the rice.

Slice the eggplant to finger thickness, and steam until tender. Add the wild brassica to the steamer for the final minute, then remove to its own bowl after steaming.

Finely chop the ginger, garlic and chilli. Heat half the oil in a frying pan, and fry the eggplant slices along with the ginger, garlic and chilli until they brown a little.

In a separate pan, lightly fry the tofu or fish pieces in the remaining oil with a tablespoon of the tamari-sugar mixture.

Add the brassica and oxalis with the remaining tamari mixture to the eggplant pan and toss all together on the heat until the greens are wilted. Remove from heat and fold in the sesame oil.

Place the vegetable mix on a bed of rice, top with tofu or fish, and sprinkle with toasted sesame seeds to serve.

Prickly Pear Pizza

We love this. We made it up, then we wanted to make it all the time. We made it for other people, then *they* wanted us to make it all the time.

It is worth cooking up several cactus pads at once in the way suggested here, as they keep well in the fridge and can then be thrown into other dishes throughout the week.

To simplify this recipe, use Lebanese flat bread as a pizza base and halve the time the pizza spends in the oven.

Ingredients for 4 serves

The topping

½ cup of your favourite pizza sauce
2 cloves of garlic, minced
1 teaspoon mild chillies, very finely chopped
1 medium prickly pear pad
150 g feta cheese
⅔ tin *OR* 1 cup cooked kidney beans, drained and rinsed
salt and pepper to taste
½ a lemon for squeezing

The base

1½ cups plain flour, plus extra for kneading and rolling
1 teaspoon (½ a 7 g sachet) dried yeast
½ teaspoon salt
¾ cup lukewarm water
2 teaspoons olive oil, plus extra for brushing

Method

The topping De-spine your cactus pad (for tips, see page 95) and slice it into pieces about 2 × 1 cm. Boil in well-salted water for 7–8 minutes, then drain. Soak the kidney beans overnight then cook in salted water until tender, or rinse well if using tinned beans.

The base Thoroughly combine flour, yeast and salt in a large bowl, then make a well in the centre of the mix and add lukewarm water and olive oil.

Use a wooden spoon to mix, then use your hands to bring the dough together in the bowl. It should be soft and just a little sticky. Turn onto a lightly floured surface and knead until smooth (about 3 minutes). Don't over-knead.

Return the dough to the bowl and lightly coat with olive oil to prevent drying. Cover the bowl with a damp tea towel and place in a warm spot to rise. Leave for about 1 hour, or until doubled in size.

Brush two medium pizza trays with olive oil and sprinkle with a little flour. Preheat the oven to 230°C. Divide the dough into two equal portions and roll out on a lightly floured surface to almost the size of your pizza trays. Lift onto trays and tease the dough out to the edges with your fingers.

Prick with a fork, avoiding the edges, and apply your pizza sauce followed by the beans, then prickly pear, then crumbled feta. Scatter chilli and garlic across both pizzas, season with salt and pepper, and finish with a squeeze of lemon juice.

Leave in a warm place for 15 minutes or until the edges have risen slightly. Bake in the oven for 10 minutes, then swap the trays around in the oven and bake for a further 5–10 minutes.

5 Weeds in the garden

The plants we call weeds are an irrepressible force of nature. Absolute control – that is, total eradication – is very often not an option, and you can waste a lot of energy or put a lot of money into the hands of chemical companies trying to achieve it. Read on, and discover what we think is a more fruitful approach …

Weeding is one of the perennial chores of the gardener. By discovering and utilising these spontaneous guests, we immediately give ourselves more time to stare absent-mindedly into the middle distance. But weeds' merits do not end with their edible and medicinal qualities: they can benefit our gardens too.

To manage weeds to our gain we need to first understand a little of their dispositions. While gardening we often strip and dig over earth. Exposing bare soil to the elements makes it vulnerable to erosion or loss of soil life. But naked soil is also an irresistible opportunity that plants will quickly respond to, and as they grow, they protect the soil like an ecological 'band-aid'. The *fastest* growing plant bandaids tend to be weedy species, whose abundant seed banks and tolerance for harsh conditions can help put a green fuzz on exposed earth. And that immediately begins the processes of retaining moisture, creating organic matter, improving soil structure and feeding soil microbes. If you don't want weeds to move in to do these essential jobs, you must cover the soil in some other way. But why not let them do what they do so well, and exploit them a little while they are at it?

Colonising bare ground.

Weeds as plants to improve the soil

Picture this: you have a garden with lots of bare earth, and hard, compacted soil. The soil has little structure, organic matter or micro-organism life to keep it healthy, and nutrients have been leached out of the topsoil into deep subsoil. Rain runs straight off, and any moisture that is retained evaporates in no time. Much of what you've planted seems stunted and unhealthy.

Many weeds have vigorous root systems. All weeds can help stabilise sloping or eroding ground, while tap-rooted weeds such as dock, dandelion, plantain and mallow can also penetrate hard or heavy soils, acting as nature's garden forks. Not only this, but all these roots remain in the soil and eventually decay, becoming that ultimate soil improver, humus. Decomposing roots leave channels for drainage, aeration and earthworms, improving soil texture and allowing those beneficial soil-inhabiting micro-organisms – so essential for healthy plant growth – to multiply. Above the ground, the decomposing parts of the weeds also contribute organic matter, which begins to form a mulch layer on the soil surface. In the case of deep-rooted weeds, they have accessed the nutrients from lower in the soil profile, and now release them into the topsoil as they decompose. The living weeds and this mulch layer act together to both improve the moisture retention and moderate the temperature of the soil – further helping those wondrous micro-organisms to thrive.

The taproots of dandelion are harvested for roasting: one of nature's garden forks.

Weeds as nurse plants

All living plants will moderate the effects of wind and sun, and humidify and cool the air around young seedlings in hot, dry or exposed gardens. As weeds will grow quickly and in adverse conditions, they are excellent casual labour in the role of shelter provision, and can be removed heartlessly once they have served their purpose! And no – since you asked – while we love edible weeds, our gardens aren't exclusively full of them, because there are lots of other plants we love too! But we let weeds fill in the gaps between our vegie seedlings and other new plantings, and progressively pull them out as our chosen plants grow. That way we get the weeds' services, while minimising competition for sun, water and nutrients. To keep future weeds at manageable levels, we remove their flowers before they go to seed. By the time our vegetable plants begin to touch each other, we'll have removed all the weeds, and begun cycling them through the compost, creating even more rich organic matter for the garden.

How to get rid of weeds

No matter how impassioned you may become about the various weeds in your garden, you will inevitably want to get rid of some of them – much as you would want to get rid of your favourite armchair if it kept showing up in the middle of your bed. There are many excellent organic gardening books that can tell you how to do this, so we will only touch briefly on the subject.

Firstly, remove the conditions that promote weed growth by maintaining good levels of plant cover or mulch. Much of both of our gardens – front and back – are devoted to what is known as an urban-scale 'food forest'. Strawberries, violets, nasturtiums and alyssums make a dense and colourful groundcover. Garden sorrel, rhubarb, asparagus, tansy, yarrow, blueberries, currants, acacias

A 'food forest' allows little room for weeds to grow through.

and ultimately fruit trees rise above them. The system is so stacked and the soil so shaded that there are few niches left for any weeds to sprout.

Secondly, build a healthy, loosely structured soil. This means that weeds that do appear are much easier to pull out, and as healthy soil is the foundation of good gardening, your efforts will pay dividends on multiple levels.

We have found hand removal for incidental weeds, and 'sheet mulching' for bigger areas, to be effective for most weeds in the home garden. Hand removal might be pulling the weed up, or repeatedly chopping it off at ground level, thereby not disturbing the soil but gradually weakening the weed by preventing photosynthesis. These methods are not always enough for weeds that can reproduce 'vegetatively', that is, via root or stem pieces (runner grasses such as couch or kikuyu, and rhizome fragments of

Some vegetatively reproducing plants, from left to right: couch grass, tradescantia and oxalis.

An all-ages sheet mulching event on a permablitz.

Jerusalem artichokes) or bulbs (such as oxalis). Runner grasses and bulb-bearing weeds are best sheet mulched, but much more thickly than with other weeds.

Sheet mulching involves feeding the weedy area (chicken manure is good) and watering it well. The idea here is to stimulate growth that moves some of the plants' energy from the roots into the leaves, which you are now going to suffocate. Lay sheets of cardboard (large boxes from bicycle shops are ideal) at least two layers thick over the whole area, making sure the sheets have lots of overlap at every point. Then cover the cardboard either with a generous layer of mulch or with your new garden bed.

When you have pulled your weeds, you have a decision to make about their disposal to prevent them from reproducing: compost, 'weed tea', or the rubbish bin. If the weeds haven't gone to seed and aren't vegetative reproducers, then they are simply good nutrient-rich organic matter and can be used in any way you like. Composting in this case could mean a classic compost pile, or could simply be a matter of chopping the weeds up, sprinkling them on an area that needs feeding, and covering them with some dry, brown material (like woodchips, straw or autumn leaves) to prevent their goodness being lost to the air.

If your weeds *have* gone to seed or *are* vegetative reproducers, you need to deal with them in a different way. Only a hot-composting process will destroy these, and this involves building a fresh, layered heap of at least a cubic metre, so that its internal temperature can reach 55°C. Even then it is advisable to soak vegetative reproducers in a barrel of water for a few weeks first, stirring once a day with a stick to prevent them from becoming rank. When the liquid has become deeply coloured, strain it off, and you have made 'weed tea'. Dilute this until it has the colour intensity of apple juice, and use it to water plants and to spray on foliage for improved growth and health.

If this all seems too much effort, you could throw your weeds in the council green bin, but be aware that in doing so you are stripping the soil of the nutrients that have gone into that weed. This can exacerbate soil deficiencies, and actually encourage a return of the same weed species that was so well adapted to deal with those deficiencies in the first place.

A weed 'tea' – turn the problem weeds into a liquid fertiliser.

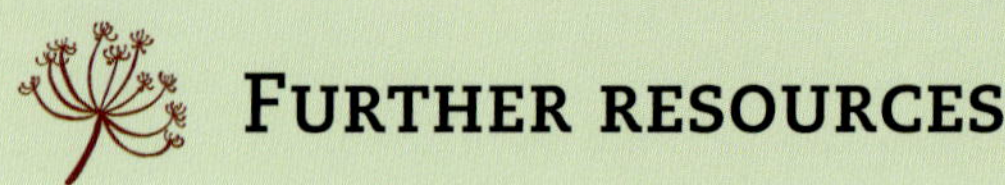

Further resources

We have used thousands of sources in writing this book. A list of our direct references can be found on our website www.eatthatweed.com, where you can also find additional photos, recipes, and details about our workshops.

The following selection of books and web resources have been particularly useful or inspiring, both over the years and in putting together this book.

Identification assistance

Websites and online forums

Note that with any of the resources that include non-expert, crowd-sourced identification, you should not accept the first suggestion that comes along before consuming a plant!

iNaturalist – an incredible community of nature enthusiasts, which is structured around map-located observations of plants, fungi and animals. Find out what's in your area, get your eye in with other people's photos, upload your own observations and get ID assistance: www.inaturalist.org

Plant Identification Australia (Facebook group) – covers all wild and cultivated plants, with generally pretty good ID help: www.facebook.com/groups/PlantIdentificationAustralia/

Edible Weeds, Wild Crafting & Foraging in Australia (Facebook group) – a lively discussion board, although correct identification of plants is not moderated: www.facebook.com/groups/255804947779277

Atlas of Living Australia is a useful website for discovering the distribution of weeds and other wild plants, including what's in your area: www.ala.org.au

Government resources can be good for botanically in-depth plant ID too, like **VicFlora** (vicflora.rbg.vic.gov.au), **eFlora SA** (www.flora.sa.gov.au) and **NSW Flora Online** (plantnet.rbgsyd.nsw.gov.au).

Us. Honestly, we'd rather you didn't die. If you're struggling to identify something we're happy to take a look. Our 'Contact us' form includes the ability to upload photos at: www.eatthatweed.com

Apps

PictureThis. There are several apps that offer AI-based plant identification. At the time of publication, this is the best one. While useful, it's far from always accurate.

Environmental Weeds of Australia. Uses a 'key' to help you narrow down the weed you are trying to identify based on observed characteristics.

Books

Weeds of the South-East: An Identification Guide for Australia, 4th edn, F.J. & R.G. Richardson and R.C.H. Shepherd, CSIRO Publishing, 2025. A seriously comprehensive aid to weed identification.

Weed foraging & ID workshops around Australia

Here's some local workshops run by trusted colleagues:

Melbourne – come to a workshop with your author Adam: www.eatthatweed.com

Perth – Annie sometimes does them here: www.perthcityfarm.org.au/workshops/

Sydney – Diego Bonetto is a wonderful guide: www.diegobonetto.com

Brisbane – David Diggles runs regular walks, see: www.facebook.com/groups/brisbaneforaging

Adelaide – Kate Grigg does fungi and wild plant workshops: wildfoodhuntress.com.au

Cultural use of plants

Books

Medicinal Plants in Folk Tradition: An Ethnobotany of Britain and Ireland, Allen & Hatfield, Timber Press, 2004. This is an entertaining source of folklore from Britain and Ireland.

Koorie Plants, Koorie People, Nelly Zola and Beth Gott, Koorie Heritage Trust, 1992. This, and other works by Beth Gott, have provided us with information about the use of native plants by Indigenous people.

Websites

Internet Archive and **Open Library** are two vast digital libraries containing out-of-copyright texts, from which we've gleaned much historical information: www.archive.org and www.openlibrary.org

Google Scholar is a subsection of the search engine behemoth focused on scientific and other academic journal articles. A search for 'ethnobotany' along with a plant name is a good way to research traditional uses from around the world, although unfortunately you will need a university log-in to access many of the articles: scholar.google.com

Foraging

Books

Let's Eat Weeds: A Kids' Guide to Foraging, Annie Raser-Rowland and Adam Grubb, Scribble, 2022. Our book about edible weeds for kids, beautifully illustrated by Evie Barlow.

Edible Wild Herbs of Australia and New Zealand, Tim Low, Angus & Robertson, 1991. Out of print, so sadly hard to get, but a very thorough book if you can find it.

Edible Wild Plants: Wild Foods from Dirt to Plate, John Kallas, Gibbs Smith, 2010. Very detailed ID and tasting notes on leafy weeds. Although US-based, most of it is relevant to Australia.

Eat Weeds: A Field Guide to Foraging, Diego Bonetto, Thames & Hudson, 2022. Our friend Diego's wonderful guide full of his photos, anecdotes and tips from his rural Italian past.

Wondrous World of Weeds, Pat Collins, Reed New Holland, 2016. A herbalist's take on her favourite edible and medicinal weeds.

Websites

Eat the Invaders is a US-based website dedicated to 'Fighting Invasive Species, One Bite at a Time!': www.eattheinvaders.org

Plants for a Future is a database of over 7000 useful species of plants: www.pfaf.org

Diego Bonetto's Wild Edibles is a useful weeds database: www.diegobonetto.com/edible-plants

In the garden

Books

Weed, Tim Marshall, ABC Books, 2011. This gives excellent advice on dealing with weeds in the garden.

Weeds in ecosystems and regenerative agriculture

Books

Back from the Brink, Peter Andrews, ABC Books, 2006. Interesting strategies for land remediation, integrating use of weedy species.

The New Nature, Tim Low, Penguin, 2003. A fresh look at the role of introduced species in Australian ecosystems.

Weeds: In Defence of Nature's Most Unloved Plants, Richard Mabey, Harper Collins, 2011. Fascinating musings on the history and psychology behind the very concept of weeds.

Websites

David Holmgren, co-originator of permaculture, is a provocative thinker on topics such as weed ecologies, sustainability and global future scenarios, with writings available at: www.holmgren.com.au

Within the movement tackling invasive species, Professor **Paul Downey** from the University of Canberra has taken an impressively practical and scientific approach: www.researchgate.net/profile/Paul-Downey

Other links

Very Edible Gardens is the Melbourne-based urban permaculture design business run by Adam and colleagues. It also offers an array of courses, veggie beds and chook systems: www.veryediblegardens.com.au

Index

Bolded numbers refer to plant profiles.

TOP 10 RULES FOR THE

1. IDENTIFY your plant beyond a shadow of a doubt.

2. PICK YOUNG Picking the fresh young leaves at the growing point of the plant will generally give you a milder, juicier leaf with less fibrous bits.

3. PICK TENDER For the same reasons as above, choose plants that look healthy and are growing in good soils with available moisture.

4. PICK GREENS BEFORE FLOWERING As with most plants, weeds often become tougher and more bitter after they start to flower.

5. CHOP WELL Many wild plants are more fibrous than cultivated vegetables, but chop them thoroughly and you won't notice at all.